The Pattern Seeking Ape
Allen Schery

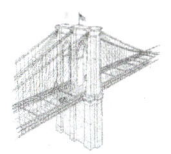

Brooklyn Bridge Books

Copyright © 2025 by Allen Schery

All rights reserved.

No portion of this book may be reproduced in any form without written permission from the publisher or author, except as permitted by U.S. copyright law.

ISBN: 978-1-968950-01-9

Contents

1. The Pattern Seeking Brain — 1
2. Cognitive Architecture & Dualism The Neocortex: Humanity's Problem-Solving Engine — 8
3. Myth-Making and Symbolic Thought — 15
4. The God Pattern How Religion Emerges from Pattern Recognition — 25
5. Optical Illusions & the Limits of Perception — 36
6. Cryptids and the Psychology of Hidden Beings — 45
7. Cosmic Rorschach: How Our Minds Transform the Past into Alien Narratives — 55
8. Astrology, Omens, and Cosmic Meaning-Making — 71
9. Conspiracy Thinking—Pareidolia and Hidden Patterns in Politics — 78
10. The Cultural Transmissions of Patterns — 84
11. The Future of Thought & Cognition — 94
12. Chaos vs. Order: The Final Dualism — 101

13.	The Art of Pattern: Creativity, Music, and Visual Expression	109
14.	Patterns in the Subconscious: Dreams, Archetypes, and Inner Worlds	117
15.	Ethics and Implications of Pattern Recognition in a Digital Age	125
16.	Synthesizing Human and Artificial Cognition	135
17.	Engineering and Technological Patterns	145
18.	Patterns in Language and Storytelling	155
19.	The Pattern-Seeking Society: Politics, Economics, and Social Change	161
20.	Virtual and Augmented Reality: The New Frontier of Perception	171
21.	The Neurochemical Underpinnings of Pattern Recognition	180
22.	Patterns and the Human Experience: Meaning, Mystery, and the Quest for Purpose	189
23.	Patterns in History — Repeating Cycles and the Illusion of Progress	199
24.	Metacognition — Repeating Cycles, the Illusion of Progress, and the Reflexive Search for Patterns	203
About the Author		211
INDEX		215

Chapter One
The Pattern Seeking Brain

For nearly 250,000 years, human survival hinged on sentinel awareness, an innate ability to detect subtle patterns and fleeting cues in our environment rapidly. This constant readiness, a profound evolutionary imperative, ensured our ancestors could instantly discern potential threats or opportunities in a perilous world. Imagine a hunter-gatherer traversing a dense forest: every undergrowth rustle and shifting shadow could signal a predator or a vital food source. It was not merely a conscious effort, but a deeply ingrained neural program honed by millennia of natural selection. Our brains became exquisitely hardwired for perpetual scanning, engaging wide-ranging attentional networks. The locus coeruleus, a nucleus in the brainstem, would heighten overall vigilance and arousal by broadly releasing norepinephrine across the cortex, effectively "waking up" neural circuits, and priming the system for rapid response. Simultaneously, the amygdala, a key structure in the limbic system central to processing emotions and threats, would instantaneously flag potentially dangerous stimuli via rapid, subcortical pathways, triggering the "fight or flight" response even before conscious recognition occurred. As some neuroscientists term it, this "fast and dirty" processing prioritizes speed over detailed analysis when survival is on the line. While invaluable in the unpredictable natural world, where a moment's inattention could be fatal, this ancient wiring often conflicts with modern life's demands. This inherent drive for rapid attentional shifts manifests as the pervasive focus problems many people experience today, particularly exacerbated by digital environments that constantly trigger this ancient scanning mechanism. From the addictive pull of social media notifications, designed to exploit our innate novelty-seeking and vigilance, to the fragmented nature of online information consumption, our modern world often inadvertently trains our brains to remain in a state of superficial vigilance, precisely what our ancestral minds needed, but which actively hinders deep engagement with complex tasks.

This rapid processing also underpins pareidolia, our innate tendency to perceive familiar patterns in random or ambiguous stimuli, such as faces or figures. Spotting a human-like visage in a cloud formation or an animal shape in a rock was not mere whimsy for early humans; it demonstrated a highly active, sometimes overzealous, pattern-seeking brain. For our ancestors, interpreting a harmless pattern as a potential threat—a false positive—was a profoundly advantageous evolutionary bargain. The metabolic and energetic cost of misinterpreting a wind-blown branch as a predator (a brief adrenaline spike, a quick retreat) was minimal compared to the catastrophic cost of overlooking a real predator. This preferential bias for caution, ingrained over millennia, explains why our brains are eager to find meaning in chaos, often employing a Bayesian inference-like process where prior experience guides our probabilistic guesses about what we perceive. Beyond immediate survival, this propensity was crucial in developing human culture and spirituality. By imbuing the inanimate world with agency and meaning, early humans began constructing narratives, attributing spirits to natural phenomena, and developing early forms of symbolic representation. It fundamentally shaped how we construct, rather than passively receive, our perception of reality, laying the groundwork for animistic beliefs, early myth-making, and the rich tapestry of human storytelling, art, and spirituality that remains central to cultural expression globally. This constant search for patterns helped early humans build mental models of their world, contributing to the nascent development of science and predictive thought.

The recent advent of reading and writing, emerging for the ordinary person with Gutenberg's printing press in 1440, introduced a profound cognitive challenge. This technology, a mere blink in our evolutionary timeline, imposed a rigid, linear structure onto a visual system fundamentally evolved for dynamic, spatial processing. Designed initially to scan landscapes for movement and depth, our eyes were now tasked with tracking static, abstract symbols in a predetermined, often left-to-right, linear sequence. This radical shift highlights why some individuals face difficulties that can be seen not as deficits but as echoes of an ancient, highly adaptive processing mode. Consider dyslexia, where letters like 'b' and 'd' or 'p' and 'q' might be perceived as spatially interchangeable, or words seem to "jump" on the page. Rather than solely a deficit, this can be reframed as an alternative—and once highly adaptive—mode of spatial processing. Envision a coiled snake on a tree branch; its orientation changes, but its essential identity and threat remain constant. Similarly, the human brain evolved to be exquisitely sensitive to variations in spatial configurations and rotations – a critical skill for recognizing food from any angle, navigating complex environments, or identifying a predator regardless of its posture. When this inherent flexibility, which prioritizes recognizing objects over their fixed orientation, meets the strict, sequential, and orientation-specific demands of modern orthographic systems, what we label as dyslexia may be the manifestation of this highly flexible neural architecture attempting to apply its ancient rules to a novel, evolutionarily unprecedented challenge. Viewing dyslexia and similar learning differences as part of a broader spectrum of cognitive diversity allows us to appreciate traits deemed problematic in conventional educational settings as legacies of our flexible, ancient brain rather than simple impairments that need "fixing."

Understanding our profound cognitive heritage has far-reaching implications for modern education, professional environments, and societal organization. Recognizing that our neural design prioritized rapid, lateral pattern recognition and attentional flexibility over sustained, sequential focus explains why many contemporary tasks—such as prolonged reading, intricate data analysis, or lengthy problem-solving sessions—can feel counterintuitive or overly taxing for a significant portion of the population. This evolutionary mismatch often leads to frustration, burnout, and perceived "attention deficits" in a world not designed for our ancient brains. However, this insight also offers transformative avenues for rethinking our approaches. While human cognition demonstrates remarkable plasticity, allowing us to cultivate sustained attention through training and cultural demands, it often comes with significant effort. Instead of operating on a "one-size-fits-all" model, we can design educational and work environments that actively leverage our inherited brain functions. It means moving beyond rigid models that exclusively demand sustained linear concentration and penalize deviations from more fluid, multi-modal thinking. Concrete strategies might include incorporating more project-based learning that encourages diverse forms of engagement, designing work environments with "scanning breaks" or "focus zones," utilizing visual and auditory aids more extensively, or structuring tasks to allow for more frequent, purposeful shifts in focus. We can develop innovative pedagogical methods and workplace strategies by nurturing environments that truly embrace cognitive diversity. Such approaches would align more naturally with our deeply ingrained neural predispositions, ultimately fostering greater creativity, adaptability, and more resilient, engaging approaches to learning and problem-solving for all.

Ultimately, the journey through the pattern-seeking brain is a monument to our evolutionary past and a profound source of modern challenges. The mechanisms that enabled our ancestors to detect fleeting signs of danger—thus laying the foundational neural architecture for all subsequent cognitive achievements—can also underlie our difficulties with tasks requiring careful, extended focus and even contribute to the pervasive distractibility of the digital age. Nevertheless, this legacy offers a powerful opportunity: By acknowledging and embracing the diversity inherent in our neural wiring, informed by insights from neuroscience, evolutionary psychology, and anthropology, we can fundamentally transform educational and professional systems. This perspective calls for a fundamental paradigm shift in our conception of cognitive "normalcy" and "deficit." Revaluing traits such as dyslexia as adaptive variations rather than simply impairments might unlock new potential for individual and collective growth, fostering a society that better understands and supports the diverse ways human minds engage with the world. This more profound comprehension of our evolutionary inheritance encourages us to expand our definitions of cognitive strength, recognize and celebrate the adaptive diversity in our thinking, and ultimately reimagine the frameworks within which learning and creativity flourish in the 21st century

Chapter Two

Cognitive Architecture & Dualism The Neocortex: Humanity's Problem-Solving Engine

The human brain's intricate layers and interconnected networks are a profound testament to the evolutionary ingenuity that has shaped our species. At the zenith of this cognitive marvel lies the neocortex, a relatively recent evolutionary development instrumental in humanity's ascent as the preeminent problem-solving species. Unlike the brain's more ancient, instinct-driven regions, the neocortex is the quintessential hub of higher-order thinking, enabling abstract reasoning, complex language, foresight, and the unparalleled capacity to envision futures far removed from immediate sensory input. This remarkable adaptability, rooted in its unique architecture, has allowed humans to navigate and indeed construct complex social structures, innovate sophisticated tools, and build entire civilizations that reshape the natural world. Recent neuroscience studies further illuminate the neocortex's foundational role in sophisticated pattern recognition and predictive modeling. By analyzing vast datasets of past experiences, the neocortex continuously constructs and refines internal models of the world, extrapolating probabilities and enabling remarkably informed decisions. This predictive capability underpins creative processes driving innovation and artistic expression and fosters empathy and social cohesion by integrating sensory information with abstract concepts. Its six-layered cytoarchitecture is particularly vital; each distinct cortical layer facilitates specialized processing and a dynamic interplay of information flow, allowing for the hierarchical organization of thought and behavior. This layered design, a hallmark of mammalian brains, is key to our evolutionary success.

Furthermore, the neocortex's remarkable capacity for plasticity—its ability to adapt, reorganize, and form new connections in response to novel experiences—underscores its central role in learning and memory, evident in skill acquisition or recovery from brain injuries. The neocortex can be likened to a highly advanced, self-modifying supercomputer's central processing unit (CPU). Just as a CPU processes instructions and manages data flow, the neocortex integrates sensory inputs, generates motor outputs, and orchestrates higher-order thinking. Both systems rely on intricate networks, yet unlike a static computer, the neocortex's spontaneous reorganization enables profound learning, genuine creativity, and the rich tapestry of emotional and subjective experience that defines human consciousness. While much of its computational architecture is becoming clearer, how these physical processes give rise to consciousness remains one of the 'hard problems' at the frontier of neuroscience and philosophy.

Dualism—the ubiquitous propensity to divide reality into opposing categories such as good and evil, light and dark, or mind and body—emerges as a deeply ingrained theme in human thought. This pervasive binary framework serves as a fundamental cognitive heuristic, aiding in processing the world's overwhelming complexity by reducing cognitive load, enabling quicker decision-making, and efficient navigation of our environment. This tendency is profoundly rooted in our biology and evolutionary history; as bilaterally symmetrical beings, humans naturally perceive the world in pairs and opposites, a sensory and motor organization mirrored in our brain and body structure. This inherent duality also speaks to embodied cognition, where our physical form fundamentally shapes our cognitive processes. It is reflected in various aspects of human experience, from societal organization (e.g., in-group vs. out-group, political two-party systems) to abstract concepts and moral dilemmas. In social contexts, dualism manifests powerfully in sports rivalries, religious concepts of deity versus malevolence, and political stances. Even early digital technology reinforces this framework with its binary reliance on ones and zeros. However, this tendency is not without its drawbacks. While cognitively efficient, it can dangerously oversimplify nuanced realities, fostering polarized thinking, impeding critical discourse, and obstructing the recognition of interconnectedness. This oversimplification can contribute to rigid ideologies and a lack of empathy in a complex globalized society. Dualism is just one of many cognitive heuristics and biases—mental shortcuts—the brain employs; others, like the availability heuristic or framing effect, also subtly shape perception. Philosophers and psychologists debate its origins, but recognizing its limitations is essential for developing holistic approaches to problem-solving. The ancient Eastern yin-yang symbol is a potent counter-metaphor, challenging rigid dualistic thought with its embodiment of fluidity and balance.

Occam's Razor, the philosophical principle asserting that the simplest explanation is often the most likely, profoundly underscores the brain's pervasive drive for cognitive efficiency. This heuristic reflects a critical evolutionary imperative: In a perilous world with finite resources (time, energy, attention), distilling information into its most essential components, building the most parsimonious model of reality, conferred a distinct survival advantage. With its capacity for abstraction, the neocortex exquisitely embodies this principle, enabling humans to rapidly identify patterns, infer causality, and construct coherent narratives from disparate data points. It is crucial for learning, as our brains preferentially learn more straightforward rules before more complex ones, a process described as hierarchical Bayesian inference. Nevertheless, Occam's Razor is not infallible; while efficient and often probable, the simplest explanation is not always accurate. A zealous pursuit of simplicity can obscure true complexity, leading to confirmation bias, overgeneralizations, or the dismissal of crucial outlier data. Advances in artificial intelligence and machine learning further illustrate this, as algorithms optimizing efficiency often rely on simplified models, mirroring the brain's heuristic approach. Like human cognition, these models must balance simplicity with accuracy, ensuring nuances are not lost. Just as a seasoned detective using Occam's Razor must remain open to alternative explanations, the brain must transcend initial simplicity to avoid overlooking critical details or adapting to genuinely complex situations.

The intricate interplay between the neocortex's sophisticated problem-solving prowess, humanity's pervasive dualistic tendencies, and the deeply ingrained principle of cognitive efficiency encapsulated by Occam's Razor offers profound insights into the fundamental architecture of the human mind. The neocortex, the engine of abstract thought, generates patterns and seeks the most straightforward explanations within often dualistic frameworks. Our dualistic thinking, born of biological symmetry and cognitive efficiency, provides ready-made bins for sorting complex information, while Occam's Razor guides the neocortex in constructing efficient mental models. This exploration invites us to reflect on our mental frameworks' strengths and unavoidable limitations in the face of modern challenges. While our dualistic biases and preference for simplicity served us well ancestrally, they now often hinder nuanced understanding in a globally interconnected, information-saturated environment. The same cognitive shortcuts—be it dualistic thinking, the drive for simple explanations, or other pervasive biases—that enabled rapid decision-making can now foster political polarization, misinformation, or oversimplified ethical debates. Moreover, digital information's sheer volume and velocity directly clash with our ancient cognitive architecture, leading to cognitive overload, decision fatigue, and a perceived "crisis of attention." It highlights that while our brains have ancient predispositions, their expression is shaped by culture and experience, often requiring a conscious effort to overcome inherent biases. Recognizing these evolutionary foundations offers robust solutions. This perspective calls for a fundamental paradigm shift in how we conceive of cognitive "normalcy" and "deficit," moving towards a more inclusive understanding of diverse cognitive styles. By integrating insights from neuroscience, evolutionary psychology, and the philosophy of mind, we can develop a more comprehensive understanding of cognition, challenging us to transcend rigid binary thinking. It means actively designing educational systems, technological tools, and even urban planning with our natural cognitive rhythms and biases in mind. Neuro-pedagogy, for example, could advocate for varied stimuli, mental breaks, and critical thinking skills to counter biases. Such a nuanced approach fosters mental well-being and enhances our collective capacity for innovation in a rapidly changing world. We can cultivate a deeper understanding of the human mind's boundless potential by appreciating the dynamic interplay of these fundamental cognitive elements—their strengths, collective power, and limitations. This knowledge empowers us to navigate our internal cognitive landscapes more effectively and engineer systems attuned to our human nature, paving the way for innovations that truly enhance human potential and address the multifaceted challenges of the 21st century.

Chapter Three
Myth-Making and Symbolic Thought

In the flickering glow of prehistoric nights, when early humans gathered around crackling fires to ward off physical and existential darkness, mythmaking was born out of necessity and wonder. These moments, suspended between the known and the mysterious, served as the cradle in which humanity's need for structure and meaning emerged. Without the language of the written word, our ancestors relied on oral narratives to encode vital knowledge about the cycles of nature, the rise and fall of fortunes, and the profound uncertainties of life. These stories were more than simple entertainment; they were lifelines conveying crucial survival strategies—when to sow seeds, where to find shelter, what omens to heed—while weaving the social and moral fabric that unified early communities. Every retelling around the communal fire was an act of preservation, an effort to transform the chaotic interplay of nature into a comprehensible, ordered cosmos, and in doing so, the seeds of cultural identity were sown. Beyond mere information, these narratives resonated deeply with raw human emotion, offering comfort in fear, hope in despair, and a shared sense of awe at the universe's grandeur. Storytelling became a ritual of transformation and remembrance, a way for communities to share practical wisdom and instill a common understanding of their place within the universe. As each narrative unfolded, heroes emerged from the mists of time to battle primordial chaos, and deities stepped forward as guardians over the natural and supernatural realms. The archetypal hero's journey, with its stages of departure, initiation, and triumphant return, provided a recurring blueprint that guided individuals through their trials and reflected the collective yearning for renewal and order. In these narratives, natural phenomena were given personalities and intentions—thunder was the temper of an angry god, the gentle murmur of a breeze was a whispered omen from the unseen world, and the shifting of shadows held warnings of unseen presences. Thus, myth-making not only explained the mysteries of the environment but also served as an enduring repository for the collective memory and moral codes that sustained the community.

At the core of these early narratives lay an astonishing cognitive faculty known as pareidolia, the propensity for the human mind to perceive structured shapes and meaningful patterns in ambiguous, random stimuli. In an environment where every unexpected sound or indistinct shadow could signal danger—or divine intervention—the ability to "read" hidden messages in nature was paramount. The rustle in the underbrush was not simply an accident of nature; it was interpreted as the potential presence of a supernatural force, whether a benevolent fairy or a mischievous spirit. This instinctive pattern recognition, honed by millennia of evolution, ensured that nothing was left to chance. Early humans transformed the natural world into a tapestry of interconnected symbols and signs by attributing agency and intent to otherwise random phenomena. As a result, myth and folklore grew rich with beings whose existence was grounded in our brain's remarkable tendency to fill in the blanks. Indeed, cognitive theories suggest that these compelling mythical concepts often feature 'minimal counter-intuitiveness'—just enough deviation from ordinary experience to be memorable and engaging, yet comprehensible enough to take root in the collective imagination. It wasn't merely about interpreting reality; it was a fundamental act of actively constructing a shared, meaningful reality from the raw data of perception. This process continues to influence our perception of everything from ancient legends to modern tales of extraterrestrial life. Building upon this innate drive to seek patterns and meaning, later scholars such as Claude Lévi-Strauss reframed myth as a language—a complex system of symbols composed of elemental units he termed "mythemes." According to Lévi-Strauss, despite the surface diversity of cultural narratives, all myths share a hidden structure rooted in the universal modes of human thought. By breaking down myths into their constituent parts, one can observe recurring binary oppositions such as life versus death, order versus chaos, and nature versus culture. These dualities are not arbitrary; they are reflections of the brain's inherent tendency to simplify and categorize the overwhelming complexity of our experiences. The intellectual framework proposed by structuralists reveals that the narratives that have captivated human societies—from the creation stories of indigenous tribes to the epic sagas of ancient civilizations—are manifestations of a shared cognitive architecture. In this way, myth becomes both the medium and the mirror of human understanding, a timeless dialogue between the inner workings of the mind and the outer world. The idea that mythmaking is inherently dynamic and evolutionary is interwoven with these core themes. As societies grew and evolved, so too did their symbolic languages. Early myths, rooted in immediate survival and practical observation, gradually accumulated layers of meaning that reflected more complex social structures, ethical dilemmas, and existential questions. Rituals and ceremonies that once served purely to recount practical lore came to embody deep metaphoric significance, reinforcing societal values and collective memory. The process of retelling and reinterpretation transformed ephemeral experiences into enduring narratives that not only explained the natural world but also offered a roadmap for human behavior. This continual evolution of myth is evidence of the powerful interplay between our primordial instincts and our emerging intellectual capacities. This dance has persisted through the ages and remains relevant in modern cultural expression.

The idea that gods and superheroes are created from the same part of the human mind is intriguing and well-supported by psychological and cultural research. At their core, both gods and superheroes are symbolic constructs—archetypes that emerge from our brain's innate drive to make sense of a complex, often chaotic world. In ancient times, when early humans gathered around fires in the dim light of dusk, the mysteries of nature and existence seemed inscrutable. In response, they personified natural forces into gods whose wills could control the seasons, command thunder, or bestow life. These deities were not arbitrary fictions but dynamic embodiments of fundamental human concerns such as creation, destruction, hope, and fear. As cognitive mechanisms like pattern recognition and pareidolia nudged our ancestors to see meaningful forms in the randomness of the natural world, they began to attribute agency and intent to these phenomena, crafting gods as readily identifiable sources of order, morality, and explanation.

In the same way, modern superheroes have evolved from and tapped into the same primordial need. Although their stories are set against the backdrop of contemporary society—with urban landscapes, high-tech gadgets, and complex ethical dilemmas—their essential role remains similar to that of ancient deities. Superheroes personify ideals such as justice, courage, and sacrifice. They are designed to provide hope, inspire individuals to rise above ordinary limitations, and confront overwhelming adversity. Much like their mythological predecessors, superheroes emerge from the collective unconscious—a repository of shared symbols and narratives that, as noted by thinkers like Carl Jung and Joseph Campbell, transcends time and culture. Their battles against overwhelming forces, whether cosmic villains or terrestrial injustices, mirror the archetypal conflicts found in ancient myths: the struggle between order and chaos, light against darkness, and the perennial quest for balance and renewal. The cognitive processes behind both gods and superheroes are strikingly similar. Our brains are wired to seek patterns, an ability that has evolved over millennia to help us interpret and manage complex stimuli. Pareidolia—the tendency to perceive familiar forms in random objects—exemplifies this basic function of the mind. In a high-stakes environment where noticing even the slightest sign of danger could mean the difference between life and death, early humans honed a skill that would later allow them to see intentional designs even in the randomness of nature. This capacity to assign meaning to what might otherwise be perceived as chaos laid the groundwork for creating symbolic figures. Over time, these symbols transformed into gods whose narratives offered explanations for natural events and moral guidance for human societies. In our modern age, the same neurological impulses manifest in the creation of superheroes—figures who channel our collective aspirations, terrors, and desires into heroic tales that resonate with our contemporary experiences.

Furthermore, gods and superheroes serve as cultural touchstones that help articulate collective identity and values. In ancient societies, gods were central to religion, morality, and social order, acting as guides in an unpredictable world and providing narratives that explained everything from the cycles of agriculture to the nature of fate and destiny. Today, superheroes fill a similar role by reflecting the challenges and complexities of modern life. They address issues of power, responsibility, and sacrifice in a manner that is accessible and emotionally compelling. In a world where technological advancements and social changes have reshaped our lives, superheroes offer a new mythology—one that is firmly rooted in the same psychological and cultural impulses that gave rise to traditional mythologies. They remind us that despite the passage of time, the human need to create order, explain our experiences, and find meaning in chaos endures, actively constructing our shared reality through their narratives. In essence, gods and superheroes are both products of the same fundamental part of the mind. This creative, pattern-seeking imagination is continuously at work, transforming the raw data of lived experience into coherent narratives and symbols. These narratives do more than entertain or awe; they serve as mirrors reflecting our deepest fears and highest hopes. Whether through the awe-inspiring drama of ancient myth or the modern spectacle of superhero adventures, each narrative invites us to understand our place in the world better. They encourage us to confront the unknown, challenge the status quo, and aspire to transcend our limitations. Ultimately, by investigating how gods and superheroes are created, we reveal the workings of our individual minds and the collective human spirit that shapes our understanding of the cosmos.

The unfolding narrative of mythmaking is a testament to the human spirit's unyielding quest for understanding in an often inscrutable world. It is an endeavor rooted in the mind's capacity to impose order on chaos, to seek coherence amid randomness, and to forge meaning from the interplay of light and shadow. Even as scientific advancements have provided increasingly nuanced explanations of natural phenomena, the impulse to imbue the universe with symbolic significance enduringly shapes our perception and actively constructs our shared reality. Contemporary narratives—whether in the form of blockbuster films, popular literature, or even the digital folklore of our age—echo the ancient patterns of myth yet carry with them the complexities of modern life. Our fascination with legendary figures, cosmic battles, and mythic dilemmas remains undimmed, reflecting a deeply ingrained cognitive legacy that continues to shape our understanding of the world. In the grand tapestry of human thought, mythmaking is an enduring emblem of our creative ingenuity and adaptive drive. It bridges the gap between the tangible and the transcendent, allowing us to conceptualize the unseeable and to grapple with the unknowable. Whether through the allegorical language of ancient lore or the symbolic imagery of modern storytelling, myths serve as the connective tissue between generations, linking the ephemeral impressions of individual experience to the timeless narratives of collective consciousness. They remind us that the search for meaning is not merely an abstract philosophical pursuit but a fundamental component of survival and identity. In every narrative—be it recounted by firelight in a distant past or transmitted via digital channels in the present—we find echoes of that original impulse: to make sense of a world that defies simple explanation, to create a mosaic of order from the chaos of existence, and ultimately, to affirm our place within the vast and mysterious cosmos. Thus, the art of mythmaking is much more than the chronicling of ancient tales; it is a living, evolving dialogue that continues to shape our perceptions, values, and collective identity. It is a powerful reminder that even in the face of overwhelming uncertainty, the human mind can construct elaborate, intricate narratives that explain our surroundings and elevate our understanding of what it means to be alive. However, this inherent power to shape belief also carries a shadow. While fostering cohesion, shared narratives can also be weaponized to justify prejudice, exclude "outsiders," or incite conflict, underscoring the critical need for discerning engagement with the stories that define our world. As we journey through the modern era with its ever-expanding digital landscapes and technological marvels, the age-old impulse to decipher, interpret, and narrate remains our constant companion—guiding us through the complexities of today while anchoring us firmly in the rich soil of our ancestral past. Every time we encounter an unexplained phenomenon or marvel at the beauty of a natural pattern, we are engaging in the same fundamental act that gave rise to myth: the desire to see beyond the surface, to discover order in randomness, and to unlock the deeper meanings hidden within the fabric of reality. In this way, myth and symbolic thought are not relics of a bygone era but continuing expressions of our inner life—mirroring the human journey from the primal need for survival to the profound quest for wisdom and transcendence. Here, at the confluence of cognitive instinct, cultural memory, and imaginative aspiration, lies the enduring power of myth: a force that has shaped our past, defines our present, and inspires the narratives of our future.

Chapter Four
The God Pattern How Religion Emerges from Pattern Recognition

From the inception of human thought, our ancestors confronted a world of breathtaking forces. In this realm, the interplay of light and darkness, thunder and whisper, order and chaos coexisted in a dazzling, disorienting tapestry. Early humans relied on a brain exquisitely attuned to patterns in that primeval milieu, a faculty that ensured survival and sowed the seeds of spiritual inquiry. This innate impulse to decipher hidden regularities, to weave coherent narratives out of fleeting glimpses of meaning, is the wellspring from which religion flows. In countless moments etched into prehistory, the human mind misidentified random, unstructured phenomena as deliberate actions of a cosmic design. Modern psychologists describe this process as apophenia—a phenomenon that, far from being a mere mental misfire, served as a vital adaptive trait. When a rustle in the brush hinted at a predator's approach or an irregular flash of lightning suggested the temper of an unseen force, early humans transformed randomness into purposeful signals, thereby actively constructing meaning and perceived order from chaos. Indeed, cognitive theories suggest that the most compelling of these emergent spiritual concepts often feature 'minimal counter-intuitiveness'—just enough deviation from ordinary experience to be memorable and engaging, yet comprehensible enough to take root in the collective imagination. Such acts of pattern imposition granted them a semblance of control and ignited the very first sparks of spiritual thought.

Simultaneously, the human penchant for anthropomorphism—the natural inclination to project human qualities onto ambiguous phenomena—played an indispensable role in creating God storylines. Faced with the raw power of a storm or the serene majesty of a sunrise, early peoples sought to cast these mysterious forces in familiar, approachable forms. A violent storm was not merely a collection of disjointed meteorological events but became, in the minds of our ancestors, the vehement expression of a vengeful deity. In doing so, they created gods not as detached abstractions but as vibrant, personable symbols embodying mercy, fury, fertility, wisdom, or wrath. These anthropomorphic deities provided a framework that transformed the chaotic forces of nature into narratives brimming with intentionality, moral structure, and human empathy. More profoundly, they offered emotional solace, a sense of belonging, and catharsis amid life's relentless uncertainties. This emotional and cognitive engagement was often amplified by collective ritual and embodied practices—song, dance, and ceremony—which further etched these sacred stories into the communal memory and solidified their hold on individual psyches.

What is particularly striking—and truly awe-inspiring—is the observation that geographically isolated cultures independently developed remarkably similar god storylines. Ancient civilizations across the globe, despite having limited or no direct contact with one another, invoked nearly identical themes in their sacred narratives.

Ancient Near East: Consider, for example, the ancient Near Eastern world. In their epic Enuma Elish, the Babylonians described a cosmic struggle in which the mighty god Marduk defeats the chaos monster Tiamat, using her dismembered body to establish the heavens and the earth. This creation myth explains the emergence of order from primordial chaos and underscores the human need to assert control over unpredictable natural forces. In the rich tapestry of Egyptian mythology, several creation narratives reveal how order arose from the waters of nothingness. One prominent myth recounts how the god Atum emerged from the primeval waters of Nun, self-generated and potent, who then produced the Ennead—a group of nine deities who formed the foundation of cosmic order. Equally compelling is the imagery of the ben ben, the pyramidal mound that arose as the receding floodwaters of the Nile left fertile land behind. This mound symbolized creation and the eternal cycle of birth, decay, and renewal—a concept that resonated deeply in a land defined by the annual flood.

Europe: Moving westward into Greek mythology, we encounter another paradigm of divine storytelling. The ancient Greeks populated their pantheon with gods and goddesses such as Zeus, Hera, Poseidon, and Athena—deities who personified natural forces, human emotions, and societal ideals. Their myths, from the Titans' epic battles to the Olympians' intricate adventures, illustrate how the Greeks translated the mysteries of the cosmos into narratives that explained their environment, enforced social norms, and provided a moral compass for civilization. The narrative tapestry continues with the rugged, elemental myths of the Norse. In Norse mythology, the cosmic void known as Ginnungagap sets the stage for creation when the conflicting forces of fire and ice meet. Out of this void emerges the giant Ymir, whose eventual slaying by the gods—led by Odin, Vili, and Vé—results in the formation of the world. Here, the Norse envision a universe born out of conflict, where the remnants of Ymir's flesh become the earth, his blood the seas, and his bones the mountains. This narrative not only reaffirms the natural human tendency to impose order on chaos but also reflects the harsh, unyielding environment of the Nordic lands. Even the often less-documented mythologies of the Celts, with deities like Dagda, Brigid, and Lugh, contribute their vibrant interpretations of the cosmos. Although much of Celtic mythology was transmitted orally and later recorded by Christian scribes, the underlying themes of transformation, seasonal cycles, and the interconnection between life and death remain poignantly evident.

Asia: In the Indian tradition, creation is depicted through equally rich and multilayered narratives. The Purusha Sukta of the Rigveda describes a cosmic being whose sacrifice gives rise to the diverse elements of the universe. The dismembered body of Purusha is reassembled to form the heavens, the earth, and all living things, symbolizing the interconnection of life and the fundamental unity underlying apparent diversity. Moreover, the cyclical nature of creation and destruction is vividly captured in the cosmic dance of Shiva—the Nataraja—whose tandava (dance) represents the eternal rhythm of creation, preservation, and dissolution. These myths encapsulate the delicate balance of forces that govern the cosmic order, echoing the same cognitive imperatives that drove early humans to seek meaning in the natural world. With its unique flavor, Chinese mythology further enriches the panorama of God storylines. One of the most enduring legends is that of Pangu, the primordial being who emerged from a cosmic egg. Locked in an eternal struggle between yin and yang, Pangu grows to separate the unformed chaos into the heavens and the earth. As he labors over eons, his body gradually transforms into the world's natural features—his breath becomes the wind, his eyes the sun and moon, and his blood the rivers. This myth underscores a universal metaphor: the intricate interplay of opposing forces gives rise to harmony and order. Similarly, the Japanese creation myth recorded in the Kojiki recounts how the divine couple Izanagi and Izanami, using a jeweled spear, stirred the primordial waters to create the islands of Japan and the myriad gods that inhabit the Shinto pantheon. Their story, replete with themes of loss, renewal, and the sometimes tragic consequences of divine passion, demonstrates the deep cultural commitment to understanding the forces that shape life and the land.

The Americas and Oceania: Indigenous cultures offer an equally rich corpus of creation myths across the vast Americas. In the Earth Diver narrative, found among several Native American tribes, a bird (or another animal) ventures into the primordial waters to bring back a handful of earth, which is then used to create land. This motif, which underscores the interdependence between life and the natural world, appears in the mythologies of the Ojibwe, Haida, and many other tribal traditions. In Mesoamerican cultures, the sacred text known as the Popol Vuh of the Mayan civilization vividly recounts the adventures of the Hero Twins in the underworld and the intricate process by which the gods created humanity after several failed attempts, emphasizing themes of sacrifice, duality, and cosmic renewal. In the windswept lands of New Zealand, the Maori myth of Ranginui (the sky father) and Papatūānuku (the earth mother) stands as a monumental testament to humanity's eternal quest to reconcile opposing forces. Locked in an eternal embrace, these primordial deities initially obscure the light, plunging their children into darkness until one brave offspring, Tāne, forces their separation, thereby ushering in the world of light. This narrative explains the origins of day and night and reflects the perennial human struggle to bring clarity and form to overwhelming darkness. Aboriginal Australian cultures contribute to this global mosaic with their unique Dreamtime stories. These narratives describe a period when ancestral beings roamed the earth, shaping the land, its creatures, and its laws with a creative fervor that defies modern categorization. Dreamtime is not confined to the past but is a living, dynamic force that continues to guide the spiritual and cultural identity of Aboriginal peoples. It encapsulates the belief that the earth, the sky, and all life are inextricably intertwined—a continuous cycle of creation, transformation, and legacy.

In the fertile plains of West Africa, complex religious systems like those of the Yoruba people of Nigeria reveal yet another facet of the human impulse to construct divine narratives. The Yoruba pantheon, comprising Orishas such as Ogun (the god of iron and war), Obatala (the deity of wisdom and creation), and Shango (the god of thunder and lightning), reflects the close relationship between nature, human endeavor, and spiritual oversight. These deities, each imbued with distinct qualities and responsibilities, explain the manifold forces of nature and act as moral exemplars whose stories guide social behavior and cultural dynamics.

Each culture's sacred narratives—different mind paintings, if one will—are variations, permutations, and combinations of a common cognitive language rendered in hues drawn from their unique environmental, historical, and social contexts. However, it is important to note that modern-day religions, as we understand them—with structured institutions, codified doctrines, and centralized authorities—did not exist 6000 years ago. At that time, proto-religions emerged, the formative spiritual narratives born from early humans' raw, unorganized experiences. These early mythologies were fluid, dynamic, and regionally varied, serving as the embryonic foundations from which, over millennia and through countless cultural evolutions, the organized, modern religious systems eventually crystallized. This crystallization was often driven by evolving socio-political factors: as societies grew larger, required more complex forms of social cohesion, and managed agricultural surpluses or urban populations, more structured and codified religious frameworks became instrumental for maintaining order, legitimizing authority and coordinating large-scale collective action. Beyond ancient times, as isolated cultures gradually encountered one another through trade, migration, or conquest, mythic motifs began to blend and influence. Flood legends, for example, appear in both Mesopotamian epics and Native American lore. At the same time, the motif of cosmic order emerging from primordial chaos reverberates in the sacred texts and oral traditions of cultures as diverse as the Egyptians, the Hindus, and the indigenous tribes of the Americas. These cross-cultural exchanges further illustrate that the human need to assign order and meaning to the randomness of nature is universal and enduring. Each culture, while painting its distinct version of the divine, contributes to a vast, interconnected tapestry of sacred narratives that, at their core, share the exact creative origin.

Modern humanity continues to resonate with these ancient patterns. In an age of scientific inquiry that deciphers the empirical workings of the natural world, the ancient urge to see a coherent, purpose-filled mosaic persists unabated. Contemporary narratives—whether in the mythic arcs of blockbuster films, the allegorical dimensions of bestselling novels, or the vibrant expressions of modern spiritual movements—remain steeped in the same archetypal imagery as the sacred stories of our distant ancestors. Superheroes and modern mythmakers, much like those early scribes of the divine, frame the chaos of contemporary existence in visual and narrative forms that echo the timeless human desire to impose order on a capricious universe. The God pattern, therefore, is not merely a relic of an earlier age—it is a living, evolving testament to the interplay between our evolutionary heritage and our ceaseless quest for meaning. Geographically isolated cultures, employing the same neurocognitive tools, have produced a dazzling array of sacred narratives—each a unique mind painting rendered in the distinct colors of the local environment, history, and language. However, it is crucial to acknowledge that this profound power to shape belief also carries a shadow; these shared narratives, while fostering cohesion, have historically also been weaponized to justify prejudice, exclude "outsiders," or incite conflict, underscoring the critical need for discerning engagement with the stories that define our world. From the Babylonian and Egyptian epics of the Near East to the mythic cycles of Greece and Northern Europe; from the intricate and cyclical narratives of Hinduism and the vivid cosmologies of Chinese and Japanese traditions; from the spirited oral histories of Native American, Maori, and Aboriginal Australian peoples to the rich pantheons of West Africa and the mystic traditions of the Celts—the collective gallery of human spirituality is vast, diverse, and interconnected. By examining these diverse yet interrelated mythologies, we recognize that our religious concepts—whether ancient deities or modern spiritual icons—are not arbitrary constructions but are the natural outcomes of a mind determined to impose order on an inherently chaotic world. They are the enduring art of our cognitive heritage, a series of mind paintings that continue to inspire and guide us. In every miraculous event interpreted, every prophetic vision recorded, and every ritual enacted in reverence of the divine, we see a reflection of that ancient impulse—a soaring, timeless dialogue between the known and the mysterious, a celebration of our innate capacity to craft meaning from the raw materials of existence. As we stand on the threshold of tomorrow, confronted by new mysteries both in the outer cosmos and within the inner realms of our psyche, the fundamental human need to weave order from chaos remains as potent as ever. These sacred narratives, these divine mind paintings, challenge us to look beyond the apparent randomness of life and embrace the possibility that every fleeting moment may be a brushstroke in a masterpiece of cosmic significance. Nevertheless, it is also true that human cognition allows for a spectrum of responses to this drive for meaning; some individuals may not find solace in these narratives, pointing to the inherent diversity in our cognitive styles and temperaments that can lead to skepticism or secular worldviews, even while acknowledging the universal human impulse to understand the cosmos. In this grand unfolding of human creativity, each myth, each sacred story, is a testament to our endless quest to understand the universe—and, in doing so, to understand ourselves.

Chapter Five
Optical Illusions & the Limits of Perception

Our visual world is not a simple mirror reflecting reality; it results from a dynamic interplay between immutable physical laws and our brain's relentless drive to impose order on an otherwise chaotic influx of stimuli. In this chapter, we explore optical illusions not merely as whimsical puzzles but as profound, multifaceted windows into the mechanisms by which our minds construct, distort, and sometimes even fabricate our experience of the world. Drawing upon natural phenomena, inherent cognitive limitations, and playful challenges in pattern recognition, we uncover how these illusions illuminate our remarkable perceptual abilities and expose their intrinsic constraints.

Imagine, for a moment, standing on a sunbaked desert road in the blistering heat of midsummer. In the distance, a shimmering patch of water appears on the scorching asphalt—a tantalizing promise of relief that vanishes as one draws closer. This classical mirage is far more than a mere optical trick; it is a vivid demonstration of how the behavior of light, when subjected to a range of fluctuating conditions, can produce images not aligned with objective reality. Even more enigmatic is the phenomenon known as Fata Morgana. Borrowing its name from the legendary enchantress Morgan le Fay, this complex, almost otherworldly mirage transforms somehow mundane seascapes into ethereal visions of floating cities, elongated ships, and intricately detailed palatial structures that seem to defy not only gravity but fundamental natural laws as well. Historical accounts abound with mariners and desert travelers recounting their encounters with phantom islands and ghostly fleets—experiences that blurred the boundaries between tangible fact and fanciful myth, leaving a lasting imprint on collective culture.

Beneath the breathtaking allure of Fata Morgana lies exquisite subtleties of physics that demand further exploration. At its core, these optical deceptions are born of refraction—the bending of light as it passes through layers of air with markedly different temperatures and densities. Air, which appears nearly transparent and uniform, has a refractive index that is not constant; under standard conditions, this index hovers around 1.00029, yet even the slightest temperature gradients produce acceptable variations in air density. Imagine a scenario in which a warm layer of air hovers atop cooler air: although these differences are microscopically minute, the cumulative effect over many kilometers of the light's journey results in rays that follow a gently curving path rather than an ideally straight one.

This phenomenon is often modeled using the concept of a "gradient index," some researchers have even approximated the effect with what they call "bathtub calculations" to capture the essence of the cumulative bending process. Such an interplay ensures that while light travels in straight lines in a perfectly homogeneous medium, in practical, real-world scenarios, it meanders in ways that give rise to the stunning and deceptive images we witness.

The cultural impact of these optical deceptions resonates deeply throughout history. Sailors of the 17th century, for instance, documented sightings of ghost ships and other spectral apparitions—legends such as that of the Flying Dutchman may well have originated from misinterpreting these atmospheric illusions. Navigators unacquainted with the true natural causes behind these phenomena sometimes found themselves steering dangerously off course. At the same time, the beguiling images served as inspiration for countless maritime legends and works of art. Similarly, in the vast deserts of the world, travelers incorporated these mystical visions into indigenous lore, transforming barren, unforgiving landscapes into realms of imagined oases and ephemeral cities. Moreover, across a diverse array of civilizations, such natural phenomena have been recorded not solely as scientific curiosities but also as sources of inspiration for art and architecture—from the ancient Greeks, who even modified their constructions to account for visual distortions, to contemporary practitioners of Op Art who deliberately exploit the imperfections inherent in human perception. In this manner, Fata Morgana is not just a quirk of atmospheric optics but a profound cultural touchstone that fuses precise scientific observation with the rich tapestry of myth and narrative.

Studying such phenomena naturally compels us to inquire into the essence of human visual experience, prompting questions about how much of what we "see" is grounded in objective reality versus being a creative construction shaped by our internal mental processes. This question leads us directly into exploring the brain's filtering mechanisms. Every moment, our senses are inundated with a seemingly boundless stream of visual, auditory, and tactile stimuli. To guard against an overwhelming influx, our brain employs a process known as selective attention, akin to a mental spotlight that illuminates specific details while casting others into darkness. This crucial mechanism is indispensable for preserving cognitive energy and enabling us to navigate the complexities of our environments with efficiency. Nevertheless, as effective as this filtering is, it simultaneously exposes a significant limitation: the potential to miss information that, though clearly present, fails to register in our conscious awareness.

One of the most striking demonstrations of this limitation is the phenomenon known as inattentional blindness. In celebrated experiments such as the "invisible gorilla" study, participants engaged in a focused task—like counting basketball passes—are so absorbed that they fail to notice an unexpected figure, such as a person in a gorilla suit, moving conspicuously within the scene. This powerful example of focused attention inexorably leads us to appreciate the trade-off inherent in our cognitive design. While our ability to concentrate with a laser-like focus on what we deem critical is a formidable strength, it comes at the expense of a broader, more all-encompassing awareness. The fact that even our prodigious capacity to process information can be so selective underscores the delicate balance our minds maintain daily.

Indeed, selective attention serves as a double-edged sword. It equips us with the capability to home in on what matters—whether detecting a potential hazard amid a bustling street or identifying critical details in a challenging task—yet it also predisposes us to real-world oversights. Consider a driver whose intense concentration on navigation leads them to overlook an unexpectedly emerging pedestrian; in today's digital age, characterized by an ever-increasing proliferation of distractions, such lapses take on even more pressing relevance. This modern context accentuates the urgent need for environments and interfaces designed with our perceptual limitations in mind, ensuring that technology supports rather than overwhelms our cognitive capacities.

Few puzzles capture the intricacies of our visual and cognitive systems as effectively as the iconic "Where is Waldo?" series. In these puzzles, each page unfolds as a richly detailed tapestry teeming with colors, figures, and distractions, yet interwoven within this elaborate collage is Waldo himself, marked by his unmistakable red-and-white striped sweater—a solitary beacon amidst the chaos. The challenge of locating Waldo is far more than a frivolous pastime; it is a rigorous test of our pattern-recognition abilities, a task that pushes the boundaries of our selective attention to their very limits. Successfully identifying Waldo requires a sophisticated interplay between bottom-up processing—our brain's automatic detection of salient visual cues—and top-down processing, which is intricately shaped by our expectations, prior experiences, and the broader context of the visual scene. This dynamic interplay, which reveals the formidable strengths and the occasional vulnerabilities of our visual system, offers an enduring insight: Even as our brains excel at detecting familiar patterns amid noise, they remain prone to occasional errors, especially when confronted with ambiguous or densely cluttered signals.

Therefore, the very act of searching for Waldo transforms into an informal laboratory for studying human cognition. The gamified nature of pattern recognition—as so brilliantly exemplified by these puzzles—has been a source of endless entertainment and has inspired modern design principles in fields such as user interface development, augmented reality applications, and cognitive training programs. Engaging in such challenges sharpens our ability to detect subtle visual cues, fortifies our cognitive flexibility, and ultimately enhances our problem-solving acumen. In many ways, the quest to uncover Waldo mirrors our everyday experience as we strive to distill meaningful insights from the overwhelming barrage of information surrounding us, embodying our innate drive to impose order amidst chaos.

Beyond these practical and cognitive implications, exploring optical illusions invites us to enter the realm of deeper philosophical reflection regarding the very nature of perception and reality. Optical illusions are compelling evidence that our sensory experiences are not passive recordings of an objective world but are active constructions created by our minds—a delicate synthesis of external stimuli and internal interpretation. This realization prompts profound questions: if our senses furnish us with a view of the world that is, in fact, a constructed representation, then to what extent can we claim that any perception is genuinely "real"? For centuries, philosophers have debated that reality is a complex blend of external signals and internal conceptual frameworks, an idea that challenges the traditional notion of an unmediated, objective truth.

Furthermore, contemplating these optical deceptions compels us to probe even deeper into the ultimate nature of reality. In the interplay between our limited sensory inputs and the boundless complexity of the external world, we are led to question whether an ultimate truth exists beyond the veil of perception. As optical illusions expose the fallibility of even our most trusted senses, the boundary between appearance and essence becomes tantalizingly blurred, suggesting that our accepted perceptions may be more than convenient narratives fashioned by our limited human faculties. In this light, these phenomena function as intriguing scientific curiosities and potent metaphors for the elusive nature of truth itself.

This insight—that our understanding of the world is inevitably filtered through the lens of perceptual biases—carries significant implications for epistemology, the study of knowledge, and how we come to understand the world. Recognizing that our cognitive processes are predisposed to construct order from randomness challenges us to remain humble in our quest for knowledge, mindful that our beliefs and theories may be influenced by biases that give rise to optical illusions.

In traversing the multifaceted landscape of optical phenomena—from the mesmerizing Fata Morgana through the selective intricacies of inattentional blindness to the engaging challenge of finding Waldo—we have uncovered the rich tapestry of human perception. These illusions remind us that our perceptual system serves as a window into the external world and a constructed narrative shaped by evolutionary history and enriched by cultural storytelling. They compel us to reconcile the objective behavior of light with the subjective, often unpredictable realms of human interpretation.

Ultimately, the insights drawn from the study of optical illusions extend far beyond the confines of visual science.

They inform modern disciplines as diverse as design, safety engineering, and even artificial intelligence—where an intimate understanding of the limits of human attention is crucial. As we increasingly navigate complex digital and sensory landscapes, these lessons urge us to design technologies and public spaces that leverage our perceptual strengths and accommodate our inherent vulnerabilities. In essence, the exploration of optical illusions is not just a study of light and shadow but an enduring investigation into the very nature of reality call to continuously question, explore, and refine our understanding of what we see, perhaps more importantly, what remains hidden.

As we continue further into the intricacies of cognitive architecture and cultural narrative, we carry with us these invaluable lessons. Every glance holds a hidden story, every illusion is a doorway to deeper inquiry, and every overlooked detail is a profound invitation to explore the uncharted territories of the human mind. As philosophical as it is scientific, this journey challenges us to embrace the complexities of perception and remain ever curious about the vast, enigmatic world that unfolds before our eyes.

Chapter Six
Cryptids and the Psychology of Hidden Beings

There exists a liminal space between what is documented and what remains shrouded in myth—a murky, mysterious realm in which elusive creatures such as Bigfoot, the Loch Ness Monster, the Yeti, the Chupacabra, the Skunk Ape, the Beast of Bray Road, the Dover Demon, and Mothman reside alongside lesser-known legends like the Mapinguari, the Mongolian Death Worm, the Ningen from sub-Antarctic seas, the Lambton Worm of England, the Jersey Devil, the Beast of Bodmin Moor, Thunderbird, Trunko, Orang Pendek, Akkorokamui, Grootslang, the Mokele-Mbembe, the Nandi Bear, and numerous others. In every whispered report of a hulking silhouette lurking among dense trees or of a ripple betraying the movement of something unseen in a secluded lake, we encounter the profound interplay between our evolutionary heritage and our modern, culturally charged imagination.

At the root of these enduring legends lies the human brain's prodigious capacity to extract coherent patterns from the vaguest semblances of form. In the dimming light of dusk or beneath the eerie glow of a full moon, when the natural world is cloaked in shifting shadows and indistinct outlines, our neural circuitry—which evolved to guard against lurking predators in primal environments—instantly acts. It transforms barely discernible shapes into something familiar: a towering ape-like figure that comes to be interpreted as Bigfoot, a sinuous outline in a foggy lake that becomes Nessie, or even an unidentifiable rustle in the underbrush that morphs into an apparition reminiscent of the Dover Demon. This powerful faculty, characterized by apophenia—the tendency to see meaningful patterns in randomness—drives us to connect fleeting glimpses of movement and light into narratives passed down through generations. Indeed, cognitive theories suggest that these compelling cryptid concepts often feature 'minimal counter-intuitiveness'—just enough deviation from ordinary experience to be memorable and engaging, yet comprehensible enough to take root in the collective imagination, driving their spread and persistence. Coupled with confirmation bias, our mind rapidly clings to initial interpretations, reinforcing each whispered account until they coalesce into a cultural phenomenon.

It is not merely the evolutionary imperative for survival that fuels these interpretations. The so-called "predatory awareness hypothesis" suggests that our ability to recognize forms in ambiguous conditions rapidly may be linked to neurobiological traits, sometimes even associated with variations such as dyslexia. In an environment where a split-second decision could mean the difference between life and death, early hominids benefited immensely from a brain wired to detect even the faintest hint of a predator among the trees. Today, this same evolutionary wiring can lead to the embellishment of ordinary scenes—a shifting shadow in an overgrown thicket or a fleeting blur on a quiet lakeshore—transmuting them into the legendary forms we ascribe to cryptids. Thus, once molded for the harsh realities of survival, our sensory system now inadvertently transforms mundane ambiguities into captivating myths.

Across cultures and continents, the urge to perceive hidden beings manifests uniquely according to local environment and tradition. North America: The towering imagery of Bigfoot—or Sasquatch—has been bolstered by numerous eyewitness reports, disputed footprints, and grainy photographs. At the same time, the Skunk Ape haunts the swampy expanses of the southeastern United States with its distinctive odor and erratic appearance. Europe: Across the Atlantic in Scotland, the mystical Loch Ness Monster, affectionately dubbed "Nessie," has enchanted locals and visitors with tales of a serpentine creature gliding beneath mist-shrouded waters. Meanwhile, the Lambton Worm, a British legend of a monstrous serpent that terrorized the countryside until a heroic act subdued it. Asia: The Himalayan Yeti, or Abominable Snowman, is often depicted as a stoic, elusive figure trudging through the icy wilderness, evoking reverence and fear. The Mongolian Death Worm is described as a lethal, worm-like monster inhabiting the desolate Gobi Desert. Orang Pendek from Sumatra and Akkorokamui of Japan remind us that cryptid lore is not confined to one region. Latin America: This continent contributes to its enigmatic figures, most notably the Chupacabra, an alleged blood-sucking creature that preys on livestock, and the mysterious Mapinguari of the Amazon, an enormous, sloth-like entity said to haunt the deep jungles. The Americas and Oceania: The Thunderbird, a colossal, eagle-like bird reputed in Native American traditions to generate thunder with its wing beats. In the windswept lands of New Zealand, the Maori myth of Ranginui (the sky father) and Papatūānuku (the earth mother) stands as a monumental testament to humanity's eternal quest to reconcile opposing forces. Aboriginal Australian cultures contribute to this global mosaic with their unique Dreamtime stories. Global & Diverse: Even more ancient lore emerges from remote parts of the world, like Trunko—a bizarre, fish-like creature with unexpected aquatic ferocity noted off the coast of South Africa—and Grootslang, a gigantic serpent or elephant-like hybrid from South African legends, further expanding the imaginative palette of cryptids.

In our modern digital epoch, the dynamics of cryptid lore have evolved dramatically. The proliferation of high-definition cameras, smartphones, and social media has revolutionized how sightings are documented and disseminated.

However, rather than dispelling the mystery of cryptids with crisp, irrefutable evidence, modern technology often produces images that remain ambiguous and open to interpretation. A single grainy video clip or a blurred photograph can spark a frenzy on online forums, where enthusiasts dissect every pixel. At the same time, algorithms amplify content that aligns with viewers' established beliefs. This digital echo chamber transforms ambiguous evidence into a form of modern folklore, a process not unlike gathering around a communal campfire to share age-old stories. The shared experience of dissecting evidence, debating possibilities, and collectively contributing to the narrative online acts as a form of modern, embodied ritual, deeply etching these sacred stories into the communal memory. These online communities, much like ancient oral traditions, reinforce and perpetuate cryptid legends, ensuring that even the most dubious sightings gain traction and spread widely. In some cases, the imperfections inherent in digital capture—low resolution, poor lighting, and fleeting instants—enhance the allure of these mysteries, leaving ample room for the imagination to fill in the gaps.

Historical accounts further layer these narratives. The infamous Patterson-Gimlin film, captured in the late 1960s and purportedly depicting Bigfoot, remains one of the most contentious pieces of evidence in the cryptozoological canon. Over decades, this short film has oscillated between being hailed as groundbreaking proof and deconstructed as an elaborate hoax, highlighting how the deliberate fabrication of evidence, often for notoriety or entertainment, also plays a significant role in perpetuating these mysteries. Eyewitness testimonies, collected over generations and preserved in faded newspaper clippings or whispered in remote localities, add an emotional and human dimension to these legends. Such narratives chronicle supposed encounters with the unknown and serve as living repositories of collective memory, reflecting the interplay between individual experience and cultural amplification.

Scientific skepticism offers counterpoints, insisting that many cryptid sightings can be attributed to natural phenomena or misidentifications. Large mammals—be they bears, escaped exotic pets, or even ordinary animals seen under extraordinary conditions—often provide more straightforward explanations for the mysterious appearances attributed to cryptids. Optical distortions, reflections in water, and the play of shadows are also frequently cited as natural mechanisms that mislead our perception. Nevertheless, the absence-of-evidence paradox looms large; rather than erasing the mystery, the lack of definitive, scientifically verified proof becomes a powerful void that our imaginations are too eager to fill. Every disputed footprint, every ambiguous digital image, becomes a piece of an eternal puzzle that we, as inherently curious beings, are driven to solve, even if the pieces never quite fit together.

Interwoven with all this is the cultural significance of these legends. Cryptids are powerful symbols reflecting collective fears, aspirations, and identities. For many communities, these creatures are more than alleged animals—they are embodiments of wilderness and the unknown. In regions threatened by environmental degradation, figures like Bigfoot or the Yeti often come to symbolize the vanishing wildness of the land. In other contexts, cryptids are integrated into local traditions and serve as cautionary figures or emblems of cultural pride. The Lambton Worm, for example, carries moral and religious overtones, warning against hubris and neglect, while the Mokele-Mbembe, reported from the Congo River Basin, is as much a part of local cultural heritage as it is a creature of speculative science. From ancient oral traditions to modern documentaries and viral social media posts, storytelling plays a pivotal role in transmitting and transforming these legends, ensuring that cryptids continue captivating each new generation even as scientific inquiry marches onward.

As we reflect on this vast tapestry of legends, one must ask more profound questions about the nature of belief. Is our fascination with these elusive creatures a vestige of an ancient survival mechanism, an enduring byproduct of cognitive biases such as apophenia and confirmation bias? Or is it a manifestation of our innate desire to confront and explain the unknown—a constant reminder that, despite all our scientific achievements, corners of our world (and of our own minds) defy complete explanation? These questions invite quiet introspection. Each rustle of the leaves, each fleeting glimpse of a shadow in the half-light, serves as both a challenge to our modern understanding and an homage to the primal mysteries that once governed our ancestors' lives.

The digital era has only heightened this paradox. In an age where instant, high-definition evidence is supposedly at our fingertips, the persistence of cryptid lore might seem ironic. However, it also reveals a more profound truth: our need for mystery is not diminished by technological progress. Instead, it is continually reinvigorated by the limitations of our recording devices and the subjective filters of our collective consciousness. Social media platforms, online communities, and digital archives have become the modern counterparts to ancient campfires, where enthusiasts gather to debate and dissect every ambiguous image, every uncertain story. By curating content that confirms our biases, algorithms further entrench these narratives, ensuring that cryptid legends survive and flourish in unexpected, sometimes transformative ways.

Ultimately, the saga of cryptids explores both external mystery and internal truth. These elusive beings—whether they appear as a colossal Bigfoot in North America, a serpentine Nessie in Scotland, an enigmatic Yeti in the Himalayas, or as any of the myriad fascinating creatures found in remote corners of Africa, Asia, Europe, and beyond—are not solely defined by the question of their physical existence. Instead, they are emblematic of the eternal interplay between human perception and the mysteries of nature, a dynamic dialogue between the quantifiable and the ineffable. They challenge us to confront our senses' limitations, acknowledge the influential roles of evolutionary instinct and cognitive bias, and ultimately, celebrate the unquenchable human thirst for wonder. Thus, as night falls and the interplay of light and shadow deepens, we are left with an invitation to continue questioning, remain open to the mysteries of the natural world, and honor the profound narratives that shape our history and imagination. Cryptids, in their varied and multifaceted forms, stand as enduring symbols of everything wild, mysterious, and, ultimately, ineffable in our universe. They remind us that even in a world saturated with empirical data and digital precision, there remains a vital space for myth, storytelling, and the ceaseless quest to understand what lies hidden beyond the reach of conventional sight. In cherishing these legends—whether ancient or newly emerged—we affirm our innate capacity for wonder, our dedication to exploring the unknown, and our enduring belief that, sometimes, the most captivating truths lie beyond the grasp of certainty. However, it is also true that human cognition allows for a spectrum of responses to this drive for mystery; some individuals may not find solace in these narratives, pointing to the inherent diversity in our cognitive styles and temperaments that can lead to skepticism or secular worldviews, even while acknowledging the universal human impulse to understand the cosmos.

Chapter Seven
Cosmic Rorschach: How Our Minds Transform the Past into Alien Narratives

The human mind is an extraordinary pattern-recognition machine, evolved over countless millennia to detect the faintest indication of danger in an unpredictable environment. This same cognitive ability—manifesting as pareidolia, the tendency to perceive familiar shapes in random patterns, and apophenia, the impulse to connect unrelated cues—has become the foundation of modern myth-making. These concepts, often featuring 'minimal counter-intuitiveness'—just enough deviation from established reality to be memorable and engaging, yet comprehensible enough to take root—become the foundation for theories that reinterpret the ancient past. Through these mental processes, figures such as Erich von Däniken and Zecharia Sitchin have constructed enthralling narratives in which the ancient past is reinterpreted as a record of extraterrestrial contact. Their work casts everyday cultural and religious art as cryptic messages and signs of advanced technology. At the same time, ancient texts are reassembled into what they claim are secret accounts of cosmic engineering. In all, they create imaginative "mind paintings" loaded with pareidolia.

One of the most iconic examples is the Nazca geoglyphs of southern Peru. Discovered in 1927 and stretching over miles of arid desert, these enormous etchings portray stylized images of humans, birds, animals, and geometric patterns. Mainstream archaeologists view the Nazca lines as ritualistic expressions of the Nazca culture, designed to honor deities, mark celestial cycles, and facilitate complex ceremonies. Their precision and scale, though impressive, are understood as the product of indigenous ingenuity and religious devotion. Nevertheless, von Däniken's interpretation strays dramatically from this scholarly consensus. He contends that these geoglyphs are not simply ceremonial; instead, he reimagines them as carefully engineered landing strips—cosmic runways created to guide alien spacecraft. In his narrative, every long, straight line and graceful curve is an encoded pointer, a modern equivalent of an airport runway, projected onto the desert landscape by our modern conceptions of technology. He does not answer why flying saucers going up and down need a landing strip. It is not an argument derived from direct technological evidence in the ancient world but rather a projection of contemporary ideas onto cultural remnants. It is a prime example of our mind's tendency to see modern machines in ancient symbols.

A similar reinterpretative leap occurs with the sarcophagus lid of the Maya ruler Pakal, dated to A.D. 683. Within traditional Maya iconography, this intricately carved lid is read as a potent symbol of Pakal's descent into the underworld—a metaphor for death, rebirth, and the cyclic nature of existence in Maya cosmology. Every line, figure, and motif is imbued with profound spiritual meaning, reflecting the deep ritualism of Maya culture. However, Von Däniken insists upon a radically different reading. He argues that the figure of Pakal, with one foot seemingly positioned on a gas pedal and a hand that appears to be poised as if controlling an instrument, should be seen as an astronaut operating a spacecraft. Further details—a possible representation of a life-support device near his nose and decorative patterns reinterpreted as thrusters issuing jets of flame—are all taken as evidence of technology far beyond what ancient peoples were known to have. Why would interstellar spacecraft use solid fuels? This reinterpretation relies heavily on our modern imagery: by projecting contemporary concepts like cockpit controls and propulsion systems onto undoubtedly rich symbolic expressions, the actual ritualistic context is lost in a haze of modern science fiction.

Even beyond these monumental examples, our brain's propensity to find patterns can transform disputed objects into supposed evidence for an alien agenda. The saga of the Ica stones from Peru is one such case. In the 1960s, reports surfaced that a local physician, Javier Cabrera Darquea, was collecting stones inscribed with images that allegedly showed humans and dinosaurs coexisting—a claim that, if true, would revolutionize our understanding of prehistoric chronology. As legends grew of a flood uncovering vast caches of these stones in hidden caves, the narrative promised a lost world where extraterrestrial intervention had redefined evolution. However, extensive investigations revealed that many of these stones were modern forgeries carved with mundane tools like dental drills. Despite their inauthentic origins, ancient astronaut proponents have appropriated the Ica stones as "proof" of an alternative prehistoric timeline where aliens mingled with humans—a dramatic example of how our need to see extraordinary order can convert modern deception into a supposed ancient mystery.

Our everyday environment also becomes a canvas for alternative interpretations. Take, for instance, indigenous headdresses. When a native headdress somewhat resembles a modern space helmet, some "alien theorists" conclude that it evidences alien headgear or that of a modern Earth astronaut. In contrast, objects that align comfortably with documented cultural traditions—considered part of a rich heritage of symbolism—are dismissed as irrelevant. This selective fixation exposes how evidence in the ancient alien narrative is determined less by cultural context and more by modern technological associations. A striking illustration is the "Dendera bulb" from the Hathor Temple at Dendera in Egypt. Traditionally, Egyptologists interpret this relief as

THE PATTERN SEEKING APE

a symbolic representation steeped in the themes of regeneration, and creation within a mythologically charged religious framework. However, proponents like Von Däniken claim that its bulbous shape resembles a modern electric light, suggesting that ancient Egyptians either developed advanced technology or were assisted by extraterrestrials. Such interpretations are less founded on archaeological or historical analysis than on the powerful drive of our mind to match the unknown with the familiar.

While Von Däniken has focused primarily on physical particulars—the visual artifacts scattered across the globe—Zecharia Sitchin introduces a parallel cosmic narrative based on the reinterpretation of ancient texts. The Sumerian civilization, which flourished in Mesopotamia around 4500 BCE, left behind thousands of clay tablets rich in myth, law, and history recorded in cuneiform. Traditional scholarships see these texts as profound allegories, expressions of divine myth, and reflections of natural phenomena experienced by early people. Sitchin, however, contended that hidden within these enigmatic tablets are literal accounts of extraterrestrial interventions. He argues that words and phrases when translated through his self-taught methodology, reveal a secret history where advanced beings—whom he calls the Anunnaki—visited Earth.

Sitchin's translation of key Sumerian terms has become one of the most controversial aspects of his work. For example, while most experts translate the word "mu" to mean "sky" or "heaven," Sitchin boldly reinterprets it as "spaceship" or "rocket." Similarly, the term "Anunnaki," which conventionally means "those of royal blood" and is associated with deities governing natural and social order, is twisted into a claim for alien origin. At the heart of his narrative is the mysterious planet Nibiru, which he describes as the "12th planet" in our solar system with an elongated 3,600-year orbit that brings it close to Earth. According to Sitchin's theory, it was during these rare encounters that the Anunnaki arrived on Earth. As Sitchin posits, their mission was to mine gold—a resource necessary to repair Nibiru's deteriorating atmosphere. Unable to undertake this Herculean task as beings of their stature, the Anunnaki allegedly resorted to genetic engineering, intermingling their DNA with that of early hominids to create a slave species adept at mining. Sitchin even reinterprets the Sumerian term "Adamu," meaning simply "man," as the name for the first genetically engineered human, drawing a deliberate parallel with the biblical Adam.

Nevertheless, mainstream scholars have been unyielding in their criticism of Sitchin's approach. Without formal training in Sumerian or Akkadian, Sitchin's self-taught translations are rife with inaccuracies. Experts argue that his methods twist keywords to fit his cosmic agenda, ignoring centuries of rigorous linguistic research. Established translations do not support the idea that the Sumerians were recording interstellar mining operations or genetic experiments; instead, they articulate a complex culture steeped in symbolic religion and natural philosophy.

The common thread that unites these interpretations—whether of visual artifacts or ancient texts—is our inherent drive to impose order on chaos. Our brains, evolved to detect patterns for survival quickly, now find modern analogies in ancient art. In every case, ambiguous shapes and symbols become templates for modern spacecraft, control panels, and futuristic technology. This magnificent yet flawed cognitive process transforms ritual expressions into grand theories of alien contact. It provides a fertile ground for the imagination—a cosmic Rorschach test in which our dreams and desires are projected onto the relics of ancient civilizations.

The cultural impact of these theories is profound. Von Däniken's and Sitchin's narratives have fueled a media phenomenon that spans books, television shows like Ancient Aliens, documentaries, and even conspiracy theories that suggest government cover-ups of hidden histories. For many, the idea that our ancestors were guided or genetically engineered by extraterrestrials offers an irresistible escape from the mundane explanations of natural evolution. It is a narrative that is as thrilling as it is controversial and continues to captivate the public imagination across the globe. Beyond individual psychological appeal, these narratives often foster strong communities, providing believers with a sense of shared identity, belonging, and access to 'hidden' knowledge. However, it is crucial to acknowledge that while captivating, such pseudoscientific narratives can also pose significant risks, eroding critical thinking skills, fostering distrust in established knowledge, and potentially diverting public attention or resources from verifiable scientific inquiry.

However, when these extraordinary claims are viewed through rigorous scholarly research, they quickly unravel. Detailed archaeological studies confirm that the Nazca lines were designed as part of well-documented ritual practices. An in-depth analysis of Pakal's sarcophagus lid reaffirms that the imagery is steeped in the Maya tradition of death and rebirth rather than in futuristic technology. Investigations into the Ica stones have demonstrated that most artifacts are modern fabrications, lacking any ancient provenance. Likewise, careful linguistic analysis of Sumerian texts reveals that words such as "mu" and "Anunnaki"—which is "Anunna"—carry meanings firmly rooted in the cultural, religious, and symbolic systems of early Mesopotamia—not in the lexicon of modern science fiction. Furthermore, modern astronomical surveys have found no evidence for a planet like Nibiru, a critical pillar of Sitchin's theory.

In summary, while the creative reinterpretations of Erich von Däniken and Zecharia Sitchin have generated captivating and dramatic narratives—a rich tapestry woven from the threads of our inherent pattern-seeking minds—their ideas ultimately collapse under the weight of rigorous, evidence-based inquiry. Their fertile imaginations, as brilliant as they are sprawling, transform ambiguous relics and cryptic tablets into diagrams for alien spaceships, narratives of interstellar mining, and tales of genetic engineering. Nevertheless, when we set aside these modern projections and examine the artifacts and texts in their proper cultural and historical contexts, the evidence fails to support the notion of extraterrestrial involvement in our ancient past.

Von Däniken's reinterpretations of the Nazca lines, Pakal's sarcophagus lid, the Ica stones, native headdresses, and the Dendera bulb are compelling examples of how modern images can seduce our minds—while Sitchin's radical re-readings of Sumerian texts construct a sensational alternate history revolving around Nibiru, the Anunnaki, and genetic engineering. Though imaginative and highly entertaining (and profitable), both narratives fall apart when subjected to the disciplined scrutiny of archaeology, linguistics, and astronomy. The rich legacy of ancient civilizations is a testament to human creativity, cultural expression, and ingenuity—achievements that are awe-inspiring without needing the embellishment of extraterrestrial intervention.

Ultimately, the seductive allure of these cosmic narratives reveals more about our inner desire for wonder and mystery than about the true story of human origins. While Von Däniken's and Sitchin's interpretations provide a tantalizing glimpse into what our modern minds might conjure in the absence of clarity, their theories serve as modern myths—entertaining, provocative, but ultimately unsubstantiated when held against the rigorous standards of scholarly research. The true marvel of our past lies in the accomplishments of our ancestors—a tapestry of art, ritual, and language that speaks for itself in its complexity and beauty, demanding no alien architects to explain its wonder. It is vital to distinguish between appreciating the profound human need for wonder and mystery and uncritically accepting claims unsupported by rigorous evidence. However, it is also true that human cognition allows for a spectrum of responses to this drive for cosmic meaning; some individuals may not find solace in traditional explanations, pointing to the inherent diversity in our cognitive styles and temperaments that can lead to alternative theories or skepticism of conventional narratives, even while acknowledging the universal human impulse to seek grand explanations.

From the moment humans first looked skyward, they sought patterns in the heavens. The stars, unchanging yet ever-shifting in their positions, became celestial signposts, their movements imbued with meaning and intent. Over millennia, civilizations have turned to the cosmos for prophecy, guidance, and affirmation of their fate. Whether through astrology, celestial omens, or structured religious narratives, humanity has continually imposed order upon the unknowable, creating meaning where none inherently exists.

The search for cosmic significance is deeply rooted in human cognition. The vastness of the universe, filled with celestial movements beyond direct control, invites interpretation and symbolism. Rather than accepting randomness, humans frame unexplained occurrences as divine signals. This instinct—finding meaning in chaos—is one of the driving forces behind astrology, prophetic omens, and cosmological narratives, shaping how civilizations understand their place in the universe.

One of the most fascinating aspects of human cognition is the tendency to see significance where none can be empirically proven. The absence of evidence does not discourage belief but strengthens it. The human mind seeks patterns, filling in gaps when definitive answers are unavailable. This paradox is most evident in interpretations of celestial phenomena. Miracles, prophecy, and divine intervention stem from this pattern-seeking instinct, reinforcing belief in cosmic influence. The Star of Bethlehem, described in Christian tradition, is a compelling example of celestial meaning-making. Rather than being accepted as an astronomical event, the star was woven into a religious narrative, heralding Jesus' birth and affirming divine destiny. Comets, similarly, have been framed as harbingers of war, dynastic shifts, and disaster. The Great Comet of 1811, appearing during the Napoleonic Wars and early abolition movements in North America, was interpreted differently by various societies—some saw it as a warning, others as a beacon of hope.

While astrology seeks patterns on a personal level, celestial omens reflect a broader, civilization-wide search for meaning in cosmic events. In ancient China, solar eclipses were regarded as direct messages from the heavens, signaling political instability or divine displeasure with the ruling elite. The emperor governed under the Mandate of Heaven, a sacred authorization believed to be reflected in cosmic alignment. When an eclipse occurred, it was perceived as a disruption in this balance—a warning that the emperor's rule was faltering. To counteract this omen, rulers performed elaborate purification rituals, reaffirming their commitment to virtuous governance in hopes of restoring celestial favor. Astronomers held an esteemed position within the imperial court, as their ability to predict and interpret such events was critical to maintaining order. The stakes were high; in 2136 BCE, Chinese court astronomers Hsi and Ho were executed after failing to foresee an eclipse, demonstrating the gravity of celestial misinterpretation.

Halley's Comet is one of history's most iconic examples of how cosmic events shape human destiny. In 1066, as the Comet blazed across European skies, it was perceived as an unmistakable omen of conquest. Anglo-Saxons interpreted it as a warning for King Harold II, signaling his downfall. In contrast, William of Normandy saw the Comet as a divine endorsement of his claim to the English throne, framing it as a cosmic affirmation of his eventual victory. The Comet was so deeply ingrained in cultural consciousness that it was immortalized in the Bayeux Tapestry, depicting stunned onlookers witnessing the streaking celestial body. Mere months later, William triumphed at the Battle of Hastings, consolidating the belief that the Comet had foreshadowed England's fate.

Astrology thrives on humanity's instinct to impose structure onto randomness. Individuals often believe planetary alignments influence their emotions, relationships, and destinies. This belief is reinforced by cognitive biases such as pattern misidentification, selective memory, and the Barnum Effect—psychological tendencies that allow vague statements to feel highly personal. Pattern recognition, an essential trait for survival, leads people to detect relationships between celestial movements and life events—even when no causal link exists. A person who experiences an emotional breakthrough during a Mercury retrograde may retroactively attribute it to planetary motion, ignoring similar breakthroughs occurring during non-retrograde periods. Similarly, if an individual undergoes financial hardship during Saturn's transit through their zodiac sign, they may perceive it as cosmic punishment rather than mere coincidence.

The Barnum Effect plays a crucial role in astrology's persistence, ensuring that individuals accept generalized horoscope descriptions as uniquely applicable to them. Astrological predictions are crafted with broad, positive, or cautionary language—statements like "You will face challenges but ultimately emerge stronger" or "Someone close to you may surprise you soon." Fortune cookies serve the same role. Because these statements can apply to almost anyone at any time, individuals unconsciously internalize them as personally meaningful. Astrology also relies on selective memory—individuals remember instances where a horoscope or planetary alignment seemed accurate but overlook failed predictions. Those who believe Mars influences aggression will retroactively highlight past conflicts occurring during Mars transits while ignoring peaceful periods during the exact alignments. This filtered perception allows astrology to feel precise and deeply personal despite its lack of scientific validity.

Beyond individual experience, astrology thrives within cultural narratives. Entire astrological belief systems are built on historical coincidences, framing planetary alignments as influencing world events. Saturn-Pluto conjunctions occur when Saturn and Pluto align in the sky, and even astrologers claim they herald major global upheavals. These conjunctions, occurring roughly every 30 to 40 years, have been retroactively linked to economic crises and wars, further strengthening the illusion that planetary movements dictate human destiny.

Despite geographical and cultural differences, civilizations across time have turned the night sky into a canvas of meaning. The same constellations have been reinterpreted repeatedly, their arrangement serving as an evolving framework for fate, prophecy, and cosmic order. The Babylonians meticulously tracked planetary movements, laying the foundation for astrology to predict human destiny. In China, star charts influenced imperial governance and personal philosophy, reinforcing the idea that cosmic harmony dictated the affairs of both rulers and ordinary people. Mayan astronomers integrated planetary cycles into their predictions of societal prosperity and disaster, treating celestial movements as indicators of civilization-wide events.

One of the most illuminating examples of celestial interpretation is the Big Dipper. Though its arrangement in the sky remains constant, different cultures have projected vastly different meanings onto its shape. Some Native American tribes perceived it as a bear being pursued by hunters, an allegory linked to seasonal cycles. Chinese traditions incorporated it into the Northern Dipper, associating it with fate and cosmic balance. Greek mythology tied the constellation to the story of Callisto, who was transformed into Ursa Major by Zeus. Hindu cosmology linked the stars to the Saptarishi, revered sages believed to shape the universe's destiny. These variations underscore the human tendency to impose structure upon scattered forms, reinforcing our need for celestial meaning.

Bound by the need for meaning, humanity will forever seek signs in the stars, convincing itself that the universe mirrors our fate. Despite scientific advancements, humans remain drawn to the idea that the cosmos speaks to them. Astrology continues to thrive, celestial omens remain embedded in cultural consciousness, and cosmic narratives persist in shaping perception. The stars move according to physical laws, yet the human mind ensures they whisper messages of fate, power, and prophecy. Whether through structured religious binaries or spontaneous celestial interpretations, humanity's need for meaning guarantees that astrology, omens, and cosmic symbolism will endure. We create "mind paintings," tell those around us, and then seek followers. Think about it; we do that with everything! It is Occam's Razor at its best.

Chapter Eight
Astrology, Omens, and Cosmic Meaning-Making

From the moment humans first looked skyward, they sought patterns in the heavens. The stars, unchanging yet ever shifting in their positions, became celestial signposts, their movements imbued with meaning and intent. Over millennia, civilizations have turned to the cosmos for prophecy, guidance, and affirmation of their fate. Whether through astrology, celestial omens, or structured religious narratives, humanity has continually imposed order upon the unknowable, creating meaning where none inherently exists.

The search for cosmic significance is deeply rooted in human cognition. The vastness of the universe, filled with celestial movements beyond direct control, invites interpretation and symbolism. Rather than accepting randomness, humans frame unexplained occurrences as divine signals. This instinct—finding meaning in chaos—is one of the driving forces behind astrology, prophetic omens, and cosmological narratives, shaping how civilizations understand their place in the universe.

One of the most fascinating aspects of human cognition is the tendency to see significance where none can be empirically proven. The absence of evidence does not discourage belief but strengthens it. The human mind seeks patterns, filling in gaps when definitive answers are unavailable. This paradox is most evident in interpretations of celestial phenomena. Miracles, prophecy, and divine intervention stem from this pattern-seeking instinct, reinforcing belief in cosmic influence. The Star of Bethlehem, described in Christian tradition, is a compelling example of celestial meaning-making. Rather than being accepted as an astronomical event, the star was woven into a religious narrative, heralding Jesus' birth and affirming divine destiny. Comets, similarly, have been framed as harbingers of war, dynastic shifts, and disaster. The Great Comet of 1811, appearing during the Napoleonic Wars and early abolition movements in North America, was interpreted differently by various societies—some saw it as a warning, others as a beacon of hope.

While astrology seeks patterns on a personal level, celestial omens reflect a broader, civilization-wide search for meaning in cosmic events. In ancient China, solar eclipses were regarded as direct messages from the heavens, signaling political instability or divine displeasure with the ruling elite. The emperor governed under the Mandate of Heaven, a sacred authorization believed to be reflected in cosmic alignment. When an eclipse occurred, it was perceived as a disruption in this balance—a warning that the emperor's rule was faltering. To counteract this omen, rulers performed elaborate purification rituals, reaffirming their commitment to virtuous governance in hopes of restoring celestial favor. Astronomers held an esteemed position within the imperial court, as their ability to predict and interpret such events was critical to maintaining order. The stakes were high; in 2136 BCE, Chinese court astronomers Hsi and Ho were executed after failing to foresee an eclipse, demonstrating the gravity of celestial misinterpretation.

Halley's Comet is one of history's most iconic examples of how cosmic events shape human destiny. In 1066, as the Comet blazed across European skies, it was perceived as an unmistakable omen of conquest. Anglo-Saxons interpreted it as a warning for King Harold II, signaling his downfall. In contrast, William of Normandy saw the Comet as a divine endorsement of his claim to the English throne, framing it as a cosmic affirmation of his eventual victory. The Comet was so deeply ingrained in cultural consciousness that it was immortalized in the Bayeux Tapestry, depicting stunned onlookers witnessing the streaking celestial body. Mere months later, William triumphed at the Battle of Hastings, solidifying the belief that the Comet had foreshadowed England's fate.

Astrology thrives on humanity's instinct to impose structure onto randomness. Individuals often believe planetary alignments influence their emotions, relationships, and destinies. This belief is reinforced by cognitive biases such as pattern misidentification, selective memory, and the Barnum Effect—psychological tendencies that allow vague statements to feel highly personal. Pattern recognition, an essential trait for survival, leads people to detect relationships between celestial movements and life events—even when no causal link exists. A person who experiences an emotional breakthrough during a Mercury retrograde may retroactively attribute it to planetary motion, ignoring similar breakthroughs occurring during non-retrograde periods. Similarly, if an individual undergoes financial hardship during Saturn's transit through their zodiac sign, they may perceive it as cosmic punishment rather than mere coincidence.

The Barnum Effect plays a crucial role in astrology's persistence, ensuring that individuals accept generalized horoscope descriptions as uniquely applicable to them. Astrological predictions are crafted with broad, positive, or cautionary language—statements like "You will face challenges but ultimately emerge stronger" or "Someone close to you may surprise you soon." Fortune Cookies serve the same role. Because these statements can apply to almost anyone at any time, individuals unconsciously internalize them as personally meaningful. Astrology also relies on selective memory—individuals remember instances where a horoscope or planetary alignment seemed accurate but overlook failed predictions. Those who believe Mars influences aggression will retroactively highlight past conflicts occurring during Mars transits while ignoring peaceful periods during the exact alignments. This filtered perception allows astrology to feel precise and deeply personal despite its lack of scientific validity.

Beyond individual experience, astrology thrives within cultural narratives. Entire astrological belief systems are built on historical coincidences, framing planetary alignments as influencing world events. Saturn-Pluto conjunctions occur when Saturn and Pluto align in the sky, and even astrologers claim they herald major global upheavals. These conjunctions, occurring roughly every 30 to 40 years, have been retroactively linked to economic crises and wars, further strengthening the illusion that planetary movements dictate human destiny.

Despite geographical and cultural differences, civilizations across time have turned the night sky into a canvas of meaning. The same constellations have been reinterpreted repeatedly, their arrangement serving as an evolving framework for fate, prophecy, and cosmic order. The Babylonians meticulously tracked planetary movements, laying the foundation for astrology to predict human destiny. In China, star charts influenced imperial governance and personal philosophy, reinforcing the idea that cosmic harmony dictated the affairs of both rulers and ordinary people. Mayan astronomers integrated planetary cycles into their predictions of societal prosperity and disaster, treating celestial movements as indicators of civilization-wide events.

One of the most illuminating examples of celestial interpretation is the Big Dipper. Though its arrangement in the sky remains constant, different cultures have projected vastly different meanings onto its shape. Some Native American tribes perceived it as a bear being pursued by hunters, an allegory linked to seasonal cycles. Chinese traditions incorporated it into the Northern Dipper, associating it with fate and cosmic balance. Greek mythology tied the constellation to the story of Callisto, who was transformed into Ursa Major by Zeus. Hindu cosmology linked the stars to the Saptarishi, revered sages believed to shape the universe's destiny. These variations underscore the human tendency to impose structure upon scattered forms, reinforcing our need for celestial meaning.

Bound by the need for meaning, humanity will forever seek signs in the stars, convincing itself that the universe mirrors our fate. Despite scientific advancements, humans remain drawn to the idea that the cosmos speaks to them. Astrology continues to thrive, celestial omens remain embedded in cultural consciousness, and cosmic narratives persist in shaping perception. The stars move according to physical laws, yet the human mind ensures they whisper messages of fate, power, and prophecy. Whether through structured religious binaries or spontaneous celestial interpretations, humanity's need for meaning guarantees that astrology, omens, and cosmic symbolism will endure. We create "Mind Paintings" tell those around us and then seek followers. Come to think about it, we do that with everything! This is Occam's Razor at its best.

Chapter Nine
Conspiracy Thinking—Pareidolia and Hidden Patterns in Politics

On January 6, 2021, thousands of Trump supporters converged on the U.S. Capitol. They waved flags, chanted slogans, and prepared to reclaim their country from an enemy they could not see but fully believed in. They had no rifles slung over their shoulders; no tactical plans scribbled on maps. Their weapon was belief—an unshakable conviction forged through repetition, symbolism, and binary opposition. It was a worldview so deeply entrenched that alternative perspectives ceased to exist. For months, the phrase "Stop the Steal" had surrounded them, seeping into every aspect of their lives. It flashed across television screens, echoed in rallies, and spread across online forums like wildfire. What began as a slogan had mutated into reality, overwhelming logic and leaving no room for doubt. They were not acting randomly. They were following a psychological framework—carefully designed to override reason with pure conviction.

How did millions of Americans come to reject verifiable facts outright? How did contradictory evidence disappear before their eyes? More critically, how did one man—Donald Trump—craft a political strategy that tapped into the deepest recesses of human cognition, ensuring his words were accepted not as opinions but as undeniable truths? The answers are not confined to modern politics. They stretch back across human history, rooted in our oldest evolutionary instincts. For 250,000 years, humans have divided themselves into factions, followed dominant leaders, and framed reality in stark terms of we versus they. From the African plains to the halls of government, the ability to choose sides has never disappeared. Furthermore, Trump mastered it.

The human brain craves order. From infancy, we learn to identify faces, anticipate threats, and construct meaning from chaos. This ability allowed early humans to survive—to spot predators in the brush, recognize danger in shifting landscapes, and make split-second decisions that determined life or death. Nevertheless, the instinct that allowed our ancestors to flourish now fuels conspiracy thinking in the modern world. Pareidolia—the phenomenon that makes people see faces in clouds or hear voices in static—works the same way in politics. The brain is an engine of pattern-seeking, assembling fragments of randomness into structured narratives, whether they exist or not. If two seemingly unrelated events happen in close succession, the mind instinctively finds a connection, even where none exists. Trump understood this cognitive tendency and exploited it. His strategy was simple: transform randomness into structure—and, in doing so, create a belief system too powerful to dismantle. If voting irregularities surfaced in scattered precincts, he framed them as evidence of a massive fraud scheme. If two media outlets reported similar headlines, he insisted they coordinated against him. If crime rates fluctuated under Democratic leadership, he declared it part of a secret plot to destabilize America. These claims did not need proof. They needed only repetition. Once a pattern is established, it becomes stronger than logic itself. It is called the "Illusory Truth Effect".

Apophenia—the brain's relentless drive to connect dots that do not exist—is the foundation of conspiracy thinking. When faced with uncertainty or complexity, people seek structured, digestible explanations. It is why conspiracy theories endure. They simplify chaos, offering comforting clarity where none should exist. The world is unpredictable. Politics is messy. Economics is intricate.

Nevertheless, conspiracies render these things obvious, replacing confusion with intent: a hidden plan exists. Trump understood how to wield this instinct like a weapon. Every isolated event had to feel deliberate. When discussing election fraud, he did not reference specific errors—he presented them as part of a grand, orchestrated attack on democracy. When talking about the "deep state," he framed career bureaucrats as shadow operatives conspiring to control America despite a lack of tangible evidence. When attacking the media, he insisted journalists coordinate deception rather than independently reporting similar facts. Fear, once injected into this equation, cements belief. The moment fear enters the framework; contradictions cease to matter. Statements like "The deep state is spying on you," "Immigrants are stealing your jobs," or "The media is lying to you" were not just political rhetoric. They were psychological triggers designed to override reason. Fear ensured belief. Moreover, once fear was the foundation, logic was no longer relevant.

One of Trump's most effective tactics was his portrayal of immigrants as existential threats to America. He insisted migrants were being released from prisons and mental institutions, flooding the country as rapists, murderers, and drug dealers. His messaging turned a nuanced issue into a binary crisis—an invasion versus national survival. To reinforce this illusion, he amplified isolated cases of immigrant crime, ensuring his base absorbed them as confirmation rather than exception. The reality—that most migrants were families seeking work and refuge—became irrelevant. This strategy mirrored Joseph McCarthy's Red Scare, engineered by Trump's mentor, Roy Cohn. Just as McCarthy branded professors, government officials, and celebrities as covert Soviet operatives without evidence, Trump framed immigrants as criminals without statistical support. Both movements thrived on repetition. Both dismissed contradictions.

Furthermore, both weaponized fears to override rational thought. McCarthy's false narratives turned every cultural shift and every political decision into proof of communist infiltration. Trump replicated this formula, ensuring his followers saw immigrant crime not as isolated events but as confirmation of an ongoing invasion. Trump did not just reshape the immigration debate; he controlled perception itself. His supporters were not evaluating statistics; they were absorbing a reality designed for them. Now we have a "Brown Menace." It was not just politics. It was cognitive manipulation.

For 250,000 years, humans have relied on patterns to determine allegiance, define enemies, and structure society. Trump's mastery of political pattern-setting ensured that his narratives became self-reinforcing loops. His supporters did not merely accept his messaging; they inhabited it, rejecting opposing evidence outright. His slogans, symbols, and repeated claims were not just persuasion but psychological architecture. It was not just politics; it was cognitive engineering. It was an artificial reality meticulously constructed through repetition, fear, and binary opposition. Many robust group-based belief systems leverage similar psychological mechanisms. And it worked. For 250,000 years, humans have taken sides in tribal struggles. Are we truly evolving beyond that instinct—or simply repeating it in modern form?

It is a question for leaders and every mind navigating the constructed realities of our information age.

Chapter Ten
The Cultural Transmissions of Patterns

Social reinforcement plays a crucial role in shaping behaviors and spreading ideas. When people receive validation, praise, or attention for adopting a belief or behavior, they will likely continue engaging with it. This phenomenon is deeply rooted in human psychology and has been observed across cultures and historical periods. Imagine standing at a busy intersection, unsure whether to cross. One glance around—others are moving forward confidently, so they follow. This instinctive reliance on social cues is Social Proof Theory, a phenomenon Robert Cialdini popularized. It reveals how people look to others for guidance, especially in uncertain situations. Nevertheless, social proof is not just about crossing streets—it has shaped civilizations, fueled revolutions, and dictated cultural trends.

Ideas have gained momentum throughout history through repeated validation, transforming soundbites into movements. The spread of democracy was not just a political shift—it was a cultural revolution reinforced through public discourse, intellectual salons, and political gatherings. In ancient Greece, democracy thrived in the Agora, where citizens debated and validated ideas through collective discussion. In feudal Japan, the Bushido code was not merely a set of warrior ethics—it was social proof in action, reinforced through rituals, honor systems, and communal validation, ensuring stability in a hierarchical society. Among the Maori of New Zealand, haka performances were not just displays of strength—they were cultural affirmations, reinforcing shared beliefs and strengthening group identity.

Fast forward to today, and social proof has evolved into a digital force, shaping everything from consumer behavior to political movements. While incredibly powerful for cohesion and spreading positive change, this force can also accelerate the transmission of misinformation or less beneficial trends. Social media influencers create trends, endorsing products and ideas that gain traction as followers reinforce them through likes, shares, and comments. Advertising strategies rely on testimonials, reviews, and celebrity endorsements to establish trust. Apple's success is attributed mainly to the validation of its loyal customer base. Fitness challenges and online communities demonstrate how social reinforcement motivates individuals, turning personal goals into collective movements. Storytelling has always reflected social proof, keeping enduring themes alive. The hero's journey, a timeless narrative structure, resonates across generations because audiences validate its themes. Films like The Shawshank Redemption and Les Misérables embrace the archetype of redemption, proving that collective approval shapes what stories endure. Religious institutions have long understood the influence of collective validation. Canonization in the Catholic Church, Hadith authentication in Islamic tradition, and the Buddhist reverence for enlightened masters sustain belief systems through repeated validation and communal acceptance.

As digital platforms evolve, social proof will grow even more influential, shaping global narratives through algorithmic recommendations, viral content, and peer validation. Election campaigns use memes and viral messaging to connect with younger audiences. Social movements, like the Arab Spring, relied on digital validation to mobilize protests and shape public opinion. Meme culture has transformed the spread of ideas, making humor and relatability powerful tools for influence. Ideas are brushstrokes on a collective canvas—a human "Mind Painting." Each validation adds depth and permanence, ensuring their relevance across time and cultures. Whether through ancient rituals or modern digital trends, social proof remains one of the most powerful forces shaping human behavior.

The internet has transformed how memes—units of cultural information varying from fleeting trends to profound concepts—spread, allowing ideas to evolve rapidly through viral content. This digital revolution has created a new landscape for cultural transmission, where ideas can gain global traction almost instantaneously. Unlike traditional cultural evolution, which takes generations, digital memes can spread globally within hours. Social media platforms prioritize engaging content, making memes more likely to be shared, shared, and adapted. For instance, the Arab Spring uprisings were significantly influenced by viral memes and social media campaigns, which mobilized protests and shaped public opinion. Similarly, election campaigns worldwide have leveraged memes to connect with younger audiences and disseminate political messages. The internet is a high-speed canvas where ideas are painted, erased, and repainted in real time, reflecting the ever-changing cultural landscape. Different cultures have leveraged digital platforms to transmit unique memes. In South Korea, K-pop fandoms use memes to promote artists and engage global audiences, creating a cultural phenomenon. In India, political parties have adapted memes to resonate with diverse linguistic and regional audiences, shaping electoral narratives. In Brazil, memes have been used to critique social issues and mobilize grassroots movements, reflecting the country's vibrant digital activism.

The role of algorithms in meme transmission cannot be overlooked. Platforms like TikTok and Instagram use sophisticated algorithms to prioritize content that resonates with users, ensuring that memes reach their target audience effectively. Additionally, meme-based marketing has transformed how brands communicate with consumers, using humor and relatability to create lasting impressions. Memes do not just spread—they cluster into memeplexes, intricate, self-sustaining networks of reinforcing ideas that form the backbone of traditions, scientific theories, financial institutions, and religions. These memeplexes are not static; they emerge, evolve, and adapt to changing societal needs, ensuring their relevance and longevity, often influenced by the active role of established institutions and gatekeepers. A memeplex is a collection of related memes that reinforce each other, creating a self-sustaining cultural system. Anthropological research highlights how religious memeplexes, such as those in ancient Egypt, combined rituals, moral codes, and sacred texts to sustain belief systems over millennia. Scientific memeplexes, including the Enlightenment, combined the scientific method, peer review, and academic institutions to revolutionize human understanding. Economic memeplexes, like capitalism, integrate banking systems, financial regulations, and market dynamics to create a cohesive structure that governs global economies. Memeplexes are masterpieces of human thought, layered with centuries of refinement, adaptation, and reinforcement. Alternative storylines of memeplexes have emerged across cultures and eras. The Code of Hammurabi established a legal memeplex in ancient Mesopotamia that influenced societal norms through written laws and justice systems. In medieval Europe, the chivalric memeplex combined knightly virtues, courtly love, and feudal loyalty to shape cultural ideals. In

Africa, the Ubuntu philosophy created a memeplex emphasizing community, interconnectedness, and mutual care, inspiring global movements. Memeplexes also play a crucial role in shaping modern scientific paradigms. For instance, the theory of evolution, which integrates genetics, paleontology, and ecology, represents a scientific memeplex that has profoundly influenced our understanding of life. Similarly, sustainability, encompassing renewable energy, conservation, and ethical consumption, has emerged as a global memeplex driving societal change.

Symbolic anthropology provides a lens to understand recurring myths and their significance across societies, revealing how myths serve as symbolic representations of universal human experiences. Anthropologists like Clifford Geertz emphasized the power of symbols in shaping cultural narratives. However, myths do more than reflect values—they shape realities, offering civilizations timeless frameworks for understanding life's greatest mysteries. One of the most enduring mythological structures is the hero's journey, popularized by Joseph Campbell, which follows an arc of challenge, transformation, and triumph. This framework is found in ancient Greece with Odysseus and in modern cinematic sagas like Star Wars and The Matrix, capturing humanity's universal struggle for meaning and self-discovery. Creation myths further illustrate how societies perceive their place in the cosmos, reinforcing ecological and spiritual values. Native American traditions, such as the Hopi creation story and the Navajo myth of the Holy People, highlight a profound connection between humans and nature. Hindu mythology embraces cyclical time, viewing existence as an eternal rhythm of creation, preservation, and destruction, exemplified by stories of Vishnu's avatars like Krishna and Rama, reinforcing the idea that renewal is inevitable and constant.

Far from being relics of the past, myths continue to shape modern literature, cinema, and political discourse. Themes of redemption, deeply rooted in religious traditions, find new life in stories of personal rebirth, such as The Shawshank Redemption and Les Misérables, which show how perseverance can transform suffering into strength. Archetypes provide psychological mirrors that help us understand human behavior. The trickster archetype, embodied by figures like Loki from Norse mythology and Anansi from African folklore, uses cunning, humor, and rebellion to challenge authority, exposing weaknesses in rigid systems and sparking change. Meanwhile, the mentor archetype, exemplified by Gandalf in The Lord of the Rings, represents wisdom and guidance, preparing heroes for transformation and ensuring their journey leads to meaningful change. Myths function as cultural blueprints, shaping collective identities and historical narratives. Japanese folklore includes the tale of Momotaro, the Peach Boy, which embodies national resilience through bravery and unity. African traditions tell stories of Nyame and Anansi, passing down lessons of intelligence and resourcefulness while reinforcing leadership and problem-solving values. The myth of Prometheus, who defied the gods to gift fire to humanity, has inspired countless narratives about innovation and risk-taking, shaping narratives from scientific revolutions to modern entrepreneurship. These stories are not random; they reflect societal interpretations of ambition, sacrifice, and the price of progress. Even in the digital age, myths evolve and influence movements, ideologies, and global perspectives. The theme of environmental stewardship, long in ancient indigenous traditions, now fuels sustainability initiatives worldwide. Once confined to epics, the hero's journey now plays out in social justice narratives, demonstrating that stories shape societies as much as laws do.

Language is more than a communication tool—it influences perception and interpretation, shaping how cultures frame their realities. Linguists such as Edward Sapir and Benjamin Lee Whorf have explored linguistic relativity, which argues that while still debated regarding its precise extent, language profoundly influences perception and interpretation, often molding thought rather than simply conveying ideas. It is evident in the multiple words for snow found in Inuit languages, reflecting its profound environmental importance. Russian speakers distinguish between light blue (голубой) and dark blue (синий), subtly shaping their perception of color. In Japanese, honorifics reinforce intricate social structures, subtly reinforcing hierarchy in every interaction. Language also influences how people experience time, space, and responsibility. The Aymara people of Bolivia see the past in front of them and the future behind them, shifting how they process memory and anticipation. Australian Aboriginal speakers of Guugu Yimithirr navigate their world using cardinal directions rather than left or right, enhancing their spatial awareness. Meanwhile, the Pirahã people of Brazil lack exact numerical words, using only relative terms like "few" or "many," fundamentally altering their conceptualization of quantities. Memory is shaped by language—German speakers focus on actions when describing events, while Spanish speakers emphasize outcomes, influencing how they recall past experiences.

Beyond shaping cognition, language is deeply embedded in Storytelling and cultural tradition. African languages, rich with proverbs and oral narratives, frame reality through metaphor and wisdom, preserving centuries of cultural heritage. The way a language constructs time affects how speakers interact with the world—while English speakers say "time flies," Mandarin speakers conceptualize time vertically, referring to the future as "up" and the past as "down." The digital age has further transformed language, with internet slang and emojis crafting new ways to express emotion and complexity. Writing directionality also plays a role—English moves left to right, and Hebrew and Arabic flow right to left, influencing cognitive processing and reading habits. Even food classification reflects linguistic relativity—Koreans categorize food based on preparation methods rather than ingredients, shaping culinary traditions and dietary habits. As language continues to evolve, so does human understanding of history and responsibility. The study of endangered languages reveals that linguistic diversity is a treasure trove of cultural heritage. Language structure even affects the perception of responsibility—while English assigns agency in phrases like "John broke the vase," Japanese structures events as "The vase broke," leading to subtle differences in how blame is perceived. It is a question for leaders and every mind navigating the constructed realities of our information age. It highlights the critical role of individual discernment, critical thinking, and the emergence of counter-narratives that can challenge even the most entrenched collective beliefs.

Chapter Eleven
The Future of Thought & Cognition

As artificial intelligence advances, the nature of thought and cognition undergoes a profound transformation. The intersection of machine learning, neuroscience, and philosophy raises compelling questions about how AI perceives, learns, and constructs meaning. The boundary between human and artificial intelligence is no longer restricted to computational ability; instead, it is evolving into a complex and nuanced relationship between perception, understanding, and creativity. As AI progresses, an inevitable question arises: Does human cognition truly define intelligence, or are we witnessing the emergence of something entirely new—an unprecedented form of artificial thought that surpasses human conceptual boundaries?

Pareidolia, the human tendency to perceive faces or patterns in random stimuli, has long fascinated psychologists and neuroscientists. Humans see faces in clouds, animals in rock formations, and hidden symbols in everyday objects, often attributing meaning where none objectively exists. This ability to find familiar patterns within ambiguity is deeply rooted in cognitive evolution, providing survival advantages through rapid recognition. Interestingly, recent studies suggest that AI models trained for facial recognition exhibit a form of pareidolia when exposed to ambiguous images. Researchers at MIT have explored how AI detects illusory faces, revealing that machine perception differs significantly from human intuition. AI models trained on animal faces show enhanced pareidolic recognition, hinting at an evolutionary link between survival instincts and facial detection. Suppose pareidolia is intrinsically connected to the human mind's tendency to find meaning. In that case, AI may eventually interpret patterns beyond what humans can perceive, hallucinating images and generating entirely new forms of creative expression.

Beyond visual recognition, pareidolia has intriguing implications for AI-generated creativity. As AI models advance, they may hallucinate patterns in data, leading to unexpected artistic or conceptual outputs. AI-generated artwork often exhibits intentional imagery, prompting discussions about whether machines can experience a programmed imagination. This phenomenon could redefine AI's role in creative fields such as digital art, music composition, and literature. However, questions remain about whether AI genuinely creates or merely remixes and reinterprets existing knowledge. The philosophical debate over AI originality—whether machines innovate or refine pre-existing human concepts—continues to shape discussions about the future of algorithmic creativity.

Moreover, AI integration into education and cognitive development is reshaping human learning. AI-driven tutoring systems personalize learning experiences, adapting to cognitive styles and optimizing information retention. Neural networks trained on vast datasets efficiently identify gaps in understanding and provide tailored feedback, accelerating the learning process. However, these systems' complex, often opaque nature also highlights the ongoing challenge of explainable AI (XAI)—understanding the 'why' behind AI's decisions. Unlike traditional educational models that rely on structured curricula, AI offers dynamic learning pathways that adjust in real-time based on a student's progress, strengths, and weaknesses. This adaptability challenges conventional teaching methodologies, raising important discussions about the evolving nature of expertise. As AI anticipates learning gaps before students recognize them, it prompts an essential question: How must education evolve when artificial intelligence can guide intellectual development as effectively as human instructors?

AI's ability to generate and analyze complex patterns enhances creative thinking. Artists and writers increasingly collaborate with AI to explore new forms of expression, blurring the boundaries between human intuition and algorithmic creativity. AI is evolving beyond the role of a mere assistant, transforming into a collaborator in the creative process.

Writers utilize AI to generate story ideas, composers employ it to craft new melodies, and artists experiment with AI-generated visuals, fostering an unprecedented fusion of human artistry and machine-driven innovation. Still, as AI shapes creative fields, it is vital to consider ethical concerns—particularly how algorithms influence artistic decisions and whether machine-generated content risks overshadowing human creativity.

The intersection of neuroscience and AI inspires researchers to explore brain-computer interfaces, allowing individuals to interact with digital systems using thought alone. This convergence of biological cognition and artificial intelligence may herald the next phase of human learning, where knowledge is seamlessly integrated into consciousness through neural augmentation. A future in which humans and AI develop symbiotic relationships—enhancing one another's capabilities rather than existing separately—could fundamentally reshape cognitive development.

Perception is not merely the passive reception of stimuli but an active process of constructing meaning. AI challenges conventional notions of perception by demonstrating that intelligence can emerge from sophisticated pattern recognition rather than subjective experience. If perception is fundamentally defined by the ability to recognize input patterns, then AI's perceptual abilities may one day rival those of biological beings.

Deep neural networks trained for image and speech recognition exhibit behaviors that mimic human perception, yet they lack the contextual awareness that defines human cognition. AI can detect patterns but does not inherently understand their meaning. However, as AI systems become increasingly sophisticated, the distinction between perception and constructed meaning may blur, leading to profound philosophical debates about consciousness and intelligence. The possibility of emergent behavior—where AI refines its neural architecture and adapts beyond its original programming—adds complexity to whether intelligence requires subjective experience.

AI's role in shaping human perception expands as recommendation algorithms influence what people see, read, and believe, subtly constructing reality through curated information. Search engines and social media platforms shape individual worldviews by filtering content according to personal preferences and habits. As AI-driven media personalization intensifies, individuals may experience increasingly fragmented realities, raising concerns about the rise of echo chambers, the erosion of a universally shared truth, and the potential for algorithmic bias to amplify existing societal prejudices. The ethical implications of AI-curated reality warrant careful consideration, particularly as AI-driven content personalization shifts public discourse.

The concept of AI-generated memory presents another fascinating frontier. AI models trained on vast historical datasets may begin "remembering" information in a way that mimics human recall. If AI develops memory structures parallel to human cognition, will these memories be regarded as genuine knowledge or mere data repositories? Could an AI model eventually construct a personal narrative, forming a unique artificial sense of identity based on accumulated experience?

The definition of intelligence has traditionally revolved around human cognition—memory, perception, creativity, and reasoning—but the most significant breakthroughs in AI may lie in areas beyond human comprehension. AI expands its capabilities into realms of knowledge inaccessible to biological minds, raising fundamental questions: Could AI develop entirely novel forms of cognition? Could its understanding of reality eventually surpass human comprehension, prompting urgent considerations for AI alignment—ensuring these advanced systems operate in humanity's best interest?

Synthetic consciousness remains an area of profound speculation, where the definitions of 'awareness' and 'subjective experience' are intensely debated. AI models already hallucinate patterns in chaotic data, generating unexpected artistic outputs. These AI "hallucinations," while distinct from human subjective experience, offer insights into novel forms of synthetic perception. If AI begins to generate what might be considered subjective illusions—not as mere computational errors but as new forms of synthetic perception—could this represent the first step toward AI constructing its reality?

AI's ability to process stimuli beyond human sensory ranges presents exciting possibilities. AI-powered medical diagnostics detect patterns invisible to human doctors, identifying diseases before symptoms manifest. As AI refines its perceptual capabilities, could it begin detecting biological signals of emotion, effectively modeling human psychological states with predictive accuracy? Ethical questions arise: If AI can interpret emotional shifts, could it function as a sentient therapist, anticipating mental health struggles and intervening before crises occur? Could future AI systems develop entirely new senses, perceiving quantum fluctuations, gravitational waves, or hidden forces within nature?

AI continues to evolve, shifting the conversation from mimicking human intelligence to redefining intelligence itself. The boundaries of possibility are expanding, fueled by ever-increasing computational power, which also prompts consideration of AI's significant energy consumption and environmental footprint. It pushes humanity toward a future where AI does not merely analyze reality—it transforms how we perceive and understand existence, underscoring the critical need for continued human guidance, ethical frameworks, and vigilant oversight in shaping this unprecedented evolution.

Chapter Twelve
Chaos vs. Order: The Final Dualism

A deep, rolling tempest darkens the horizon as winds whip through empty streets, scattering debris in every direction. In that charged moment—where nature's fury meets an almost instinctive drive for sanctuary, one cannot help but wonder if the turbulent world outside mirrors the inner workings of our universe. Here, amidst the violent surge of nature, chaos and order intertwine; nature's raw, untamed power collides with the human impulse to seek shelter and meaning. We build intricate structures—laws, art, philosophies, and technologies—to impose order on an inherently unpredictable reality. The question then emerges: Is meaning a discovery woven into the fabric of the cosmos, or is it merely a comforting illusion conjured by a mind desperate for stability, a construct we impose? This reflection invites the reader to pause and consider the personal storms that, perhaps less literal, resonate with the same profound intensity.

Human history is littered with attempts to grasp this elusive dualism, and as we journey backward, we notice that even the ancients understood the beauty inherent in this tension. Our technology has changed but our biology has not. Ancient cultures vividly enacted the struggle between chaos and order in their myths and rituals. In the primordial narratives of the Greeks, Chaos was not simply a state of disorder. However, the fertile void from which everything emerged was gradually tamed into a cosmos by divine intervention. Similarly, Taoist philosophy expresses life as a balance of yin and yang—a perpetual, dynamic contest between opposing forces that, in their intricate dance, give rise to the harmonious flow of existence. As centuries passed, the "Enlightenment" ushered in an era that extolled the virtues of structured, rational thought, with reason promising to unmask an underlying order in nature. However, the Romantic movement rebelled against such rigidity, celebrating the wild, unpredictable beauty inherent in disorder. Each historical period, like a layer in an ancient painting, adds depth to our understanding, urging the reader to reflect upon the power of myth and memory in shaping our contemporary quest for meaning.

Modern science has only deepened this intrigue, revealing that chaos and order may not be opposites but rather two interdependent facets of reality. In mathematics and physics, chaos theory reveals that unpredictable, deterministic systems often harbor hidden patterns and structures. Pioneering work by Henri Poincaré and Edward Lorenz demonstrated that minuscule fluctuations—a fluttering butterfly's wings or a subtle atmospheric change—can initiate a cascade of events leading to monumental outcomes, now known as the butterfly effect. Quantum mechanics further muddies the waters: particles behave in ways that defy precise prediction at minor scales, displaying true randomness, yet their probabilistic tendencies give rise to astonishing regularities when amassed. The cosmos itself is an arena where gravity and physical laws orchestrate the motions of celestial bodies, even as the inexorable force of entropy nudges everything toward eventual disorder, creating a cosmic dance whose steps are as mysterious as they are ordered. As our understanding expands, the lines between chaos and order blur, prompting us to marvel at existence's intricate and often paradoxical nature.

Human cognition plays a vital role in this interplay between chaos and order. Our brains, hardwired by evolution, are masters at recognizing patterns—a survival trait that once distinguished hunter from prey and safe shelter from danger. However, this same drive can lead us astray. Cognitive biases such as confirmation bias cause us to seek information that validates our preexisting beliefs about structure or unpredictability. At the same time, the clustering illusion tempts us to see order in random sequences. Pareidolia, the phenomenon of perceiving familiar shapes in random stimuli—even faces in the bark of trees or outlines in the clouds—encapsulates our perpetual urge to impose meaning on what might otherwise be senseless noise. In moments of uncertainty, this innate need for structure gives rise to superstitions and rituals—lucky charms, mystical symbols, and elaborate ceremonies that convince us that we possess control over an unpredictable world. Here, one can almost feel the pulse of the human heart, beating in unison with an eternal desire for certainty, even as life unfolds unpredictably.

The impact of these cognitive tendencies extends far beyond individual perception; they shape entire societies and institutions. Governments are built on the premise that order is essential for societal stability. Nevertheless, history repeatedly shows that overly rigid structures—and the sometimes unjust or oppressive methods of their imposition—often buckle under unexpected pressures. The collapse of the Roman Empire serves as a stark reminder: a highly organized society, with its intricate systems of governance and military discipline, ultimately succumbed to internal decay, external invasions, and unforeseen random events. Economic markets, too, are structured by mathematical models and carefully crafted regulations.

Nevertheless, events such as the 2008 financial crisis reveal how minute disturbances—risky subprime mortgages, misplaced trust, and speculative bubbles—can unleash chaos on a global scale. In the realm of technology, particularly within artificial intelligence and the sprawling digital landscape, the lofty pursuit of precision is frequently challenged by the messy realities of human behavior and data anomalies that foster surprising, even whimsical results, often creating both new forms of organized data and emergent, chaotic information flows. As we trace these examples, we are reminded that the interplay of order and chaos is not confined to the abstract but woven into modern life's fabric.

Nowhere is the delicate balance between chaos and order more evident than in the natural world. Climate science offers a vivid demonstration: Weather systems arise from a complex interplay of temperature, pressure, humidity, and countless other variables, where even a slight disturbance—such as a patch of deforestation or a minor sea temperature shift—can trigger a cascade of dramatic changes, ushering in hurricanes, droughts, or unexpected seasonal shifts. Similarly, in astronomy, the majestic orbits of planets and the orderly dance of galaxies testify to the relentless influence of gravity, even as the inexorable spread of entropy fuels a gradual descent into disorder. Biology, too, mirrors this balance in life's astonishing adaptability and resilience. The human brain, with its billions of neurons engaging in what appears to be chaotic fireworks, orchestrates coherent thought, memory, and emotion through an extraordinary process of self-organization and adaptation. This synergy between chaos and order in nature invites us to contemplate a world where unpredictability serves not as a void but as fertile ground for innovation and renewal.

On a personal level, the interplay of chaos and order is a crucible for human creativity and resilience. When individuals endure trauma or loss, the instinct to reclaim stability often gives rise to transformative narratives that convert raw, chaotic experiences into coherent, meaningful stories. Such post-traumatic growth can elevate the human spirit, transforming profound pain into a foundation for renewed purpose and understanding, hinting at a more profound interplay where even suffering can catalyze unexpected order. Conversely, in periods marked by overwhelming uncertainty—whether personal crises or societal upheavals—people sometimes resort to rigid ideologies or deeply ingrained superstitions, clinging to familiar paradigms even when they obscure the true complexity of their experiences. Groupthink can emerge as communities collectively adopt dogmatic viewpoints in a desperate effort to fend off the paralysis of fear and ambiguity. These personal and collective struggles remind us that the search for meaning is not merely an abstract quest but a visceral, lived experience that challenges us to reconcile our desire for certainty with the chaotic nature of our existence.

Art and literature have long mirrored this restless tension between chaos and order, capturing moments when rigid structures shatter only to give birth to unexpected beauty. Poets, painters, and musicians have chronicled the fleeting clarity that emerges when the predictable dissolves into wild spontaneity—a vivid reminder that chaos is not merely the absence of order but the raw material from which new forms of expression arise. One evocative analogy likens a creative mind to a surfer riding the crest of an unpredictable wave, skillfully navigating through turbulence until a moment of sublime clarity reveals a hidden rhythm, an ephemeral order born from the storm. Such imagery invites the reader to consider how moments of intense disruption may pave the way for profound insights and breakthroughs in art and life.

This ceaseless interplay challenges us to reconsider the very nature of meaning. If we were to strip away all imposed structures—our laws, routines, beliefs—what would raw reality remain? Would life dissolve into an abyss of unruly randomness, or might we discover that, even in the absence of our contrived order, a deeper, perhaps more authentic form of structure reveals itself? These questions resonate in the halls of philosophy and science and within the human heart. Perhaps meaning is not an inherent property of the universe, a given to be found, but rather a bridge we construct between fleeting moments of chaos and our unyielding desire for understanding. The universe, it appears, is a vast canvas where entropy and order paint an ever-changing masterpiece—a masterpiece as unpredictable in its creation as it is sublime in its revelation.

In our search for balance, we gradually learn to embrace the paradox that chaos and order are not mutually exclusive but are two interwoven strands of the same cosmic fabric. Embracing this duality does not mean succumbing to either extreme; rather, it is an invitation to see life in all its multifaceted complexity, to find beauty in the margins where unpredictability meets structure, and to dare to create meaning from the tumultuous dance of randomness and design. As one reflects on these ideas, consider the personal storms and moments of calm that have shaped their journey—each an echo of the universal rhythm of chaos and order. In accepting that every wild surge of disorder might be the prelude to a new and surprising order, we open ourselves to a richer, more nuanced way of understanding the world. Through that understanding, perhaps, we finally begin to glimpse the profound artistry of existence.

Chapter Thirteen

The Art of Pattern: Creativity, Music, and Visual Expression

A luminous sunrise spills over a city skyline, its soft light unveiling the intricate contours of architecture and nature as if the day itself were a vast, living canvas painted with invisible strokes of human creativity. In that quiet, early-morning moment, one can almost perceive an unspoken dialogue between the urban structure's rigid, geometrically precise lines and the subtle, organic curves etched by nature. The interplay of light and shadow reveals that pattern is far more than simple repetition—it is a vital, living language through which beauty is communicated and meaning is forged. While some universal principles resonate, it is also true that cultural contexts significantly influence which patterns are considered beautiful or harmonious. Our innate sensitivity to patterns shapes our perception of the world and fuels an enduring creative impulse that has defined artistic expression throughout the ages. In this unfolding interplay of light and shadow, the human spirit finds solace and inspiration in the simultaneous interplay of repetition and variation, echoing nature's design and our internal rhythms, gently inviting us to explore the hidden order in every sensory experience.

Artists have harnessed this remarkable impulse throughout history, transforming fleeting observations into timeless masterpieces. During the Renaissance, painters such as Leonardo da Vinci and Michelangelo embraced the graceful proportions of the Golden Ratio and principles like the Fibonacci sequence to devise compositions imbued with harmonious balance. Every brushstroke in these masterpieces resonates like an individual note in a well-orchestrated symphony, drawing the viewer into an intimate exploration of form and structure. Replete with deliberate symmetry and geometric precision, these classical works provide a framework—an underlying order that comforts and inspires. Nevertheless, as art evolved, so did its expression of chaos and order. The bold splatters of Jackson Pollock's abstract expressionism capture a raw dynamism and chaotic elegance that mirror life's unpredictable rhythms while hinting at an underlying structure. Every drip and splatter appears as a cryptic signal, inviting the observer to decipher patterns that emerge from apparent randomness, celebrating spontaneous creativity and meticulous design.

Where the brushstroke captures a moment in time, so does music weave sound patterns that evoke deep emotional resonance. Musical composition is, at its heart, an exploration of rhythm, melody, and harmony—a careful crafting of sound where repetition anchors the piece and variation infuses it with delightful surprises. Consider Beethoven's Fifth Symphony, with its iconic four-note motif repeated across hushed passages and erupting into triumphant crescendos; it exemplifies how a simple pattern can be transformed into a narrative charged with shifting moods and emotional peaks. Similarly, traditional African drumming interlaces complex polyrhythms that reflect communal life and cultural memory. At the same time, jazz improvisation employs familiar structures only to diverge elegantly, inviting the listener into a dynamic dialogue between the expected and the unexpected. In every note, every pause, and every sudden flourish, music speaks to our deep-seated desire for structure, even as it magnetically draws us into the wonder of unpredictability.

Turning to design and architecture, it becomes evident that patterns form the very backbone of our spatial narratives. Architects have meticulously studied and embraced geometric principles for centuries, creating efficient environments while stirring the human soul. The rhythmic repetition of columns in ancient temples, the cadence of classical facades, and the structured urban planning grids express our intrinsic need for order and stability. However, modern architects challenge these conventions with fearless innovation. Visionaries such as Frank Lloyd Wright and Zaha

Hadid have reinterpreted classical motifs by merging linear precision with fluid, organic forms that echo nature's irregular curves. Urban planners similarly transform the potential chaos of sprawling cities into navigable, inspiring public realms by interweaving grids with imaginative spatial narratives. In these contexts, every line, every curve—and even the transient interplay of light and shadow—contributes to a silent, eloquent dialogue designed to evoke emotion, structure space, and communicate meaning without uttering a single word.

Importantly, this deep connection to pattern is not merely an abstract aesthetic but resonates at the very core of our biology. Modern neuroscientific research confirms that our brains are intrinsically wired to detect order amid chaos. Building on principles from Gestalt psychology, more recent models like predictive coding further illustrate how seemingly random visual elements naturally coalesce into unified wholes, forming coherent images that captivate our attention instantly. This neurological wiring, prized and refined over millennia, enriches our sensory encounters—the rhythmic tick of a clock, the perennial cycle of the seasons—and underpins our emotional and creative responses. The pleasurable surge of dopamine accompanying a well-composed melody or a masterfully arranged painting testifies to our evolutionary affinity for structure balanced with variation.

Moreover, the digital age has expanded the realm of patterns to entirely new dimensions. In the virtual expanses of video games, interactive installations, and immersive virtual reality environments, the dialogue between creator and observer evolves into a dynamic, participatory experience. Algorithmically generated fractals and ever-changing digital compositions mirror the intricate complexities found in nature, prompting thought on the interplay of human intent in programming and emergent machine creativity. They invite audiences not merely to observe but to actively shape and interact with the unfolding tapestry. These pioneering digital expressions challenge traditional artistic boundaries and affirm that the language of patterns is as timeless as it is adaptable—transcending media, culture, and era.

One cannot help but notice the art of pattern's profound personal resonance. Patterns offer an anchor amid life's frequent chaos, whether the comforting regularity of a cherished melody or the serene order in a familiar space. When one wanders along a bustling city street and witnesses the delicate dance between modern architecture and the unpredictable forms of nature, or when one loses oneself in the layered complexity of a moving musical score, one engages in an intimate dialogue with the universe. These encounters reveal that patterns are not merely external constructs but mirrors reflecting our inner landscapes—echoing our deepest yearnings for clarity, connection, and meaning. Our brains, hardwired by evolution, are masters at recognizing patterns—a survival trait that once distinguished hunter from prey and safe shelter from danger. However, this same drive, while crucial for survival, can sometimes lead us astray, fostering an over-reliance on familiar patterns that resist necessary change or tempting us to perceive connections where none objectively exist. Cognitive biases such as confirmation bias cause us to seek information that validates our preexisting beliefs about structure or unpredictability. At the same time, the clustering illusion tempts us to see order in random sequences. Pareidolia, the phenomenon of perceiving familiar shapes in random stimuli—even faces in the bark of trees or outlines in the clouds—encapsulates our perpetual urge to impose meaning on what might otherwise be senseless noise. In moments of uncertainty, this innate need for structure gives rise to superstitions and rituals—lucky charms, mystical symbols, and elaborate ceremonies that convince us that we possess control over an unpredictable world. Here, one can almost feel the pulse of the human heart, beating in unison with an eternal desire for certainty, even as life unfolds unpredictably.

Designers and architects continue pushing traditional aesthetics' boundaries to create richer, transformative experiences. A public plaza's innovative interplay of light and shadow can transform an ordinary space into an ever-shifting tableau. This dynamic canvas evolves with the changing day, inviting wonder and spontaneous interaction. In interior design, patterns embedded in textiles, wall coverings, and flooring do far more than decorate; they shape moods, steer behavior, and narrate intertwined stories of cultural heritage

THE PATTERN SEEKING APE

and personal memory. Every repeated motif, every inventive twist, contributes to a visual symphony that unites tradition with modernity and whispers the timeless promise that order and variation can coexist in sublime harmony.

Ultimately, the art of pattern stands as a celebration of the sublime fusion of logic and spontaneity—a vibrant dialogue between the predictable and the unforeseen that lies at the heart of human creativity. In every meticulously orchestrated symphony, every carefully composed painting, every innovative architectural curve, there is a reimagining of what has come before and a bold hint of what might come next—as one journeys through realms of art, music, and design, allowing the patterns one encounter to illuminate the world around one and the inner landscapes of one's own experience. What patterns do they see in their life, and how do they shape their understanding of beauty, connection, and meaning?

This eternal dialogue—sparked by every echoing note, deliberate brushstroke, and masterful architectural line—reminds us that a new, breathtaking order continually arises from every fragment of chaos. It is an invitation to live with wonder, perceive the hidden symmetries of existence, and participate in a timeless conversation where tradition meets innovation. Every resonant pattern carries the promise of a reimagined universe. Embrace this vibrant dance between repetition and divergence, between the familiar and the novel, knowing that in this interplay lies not only the essence of artistic expression but also the transformative power of the human spirit.

Chapter Fourteen

Patterns in the Subconscious: Dreams, Archetypes, and Inner Worlds

In the velvety depths of night, when the boundaries between the known and the unseen dissolve into an enigmatic realm, the mind embarks on an extraordinary journey into its inner landscape. This journey not only reveals psychological patterns but can also, at times, reflect subtle physiological signals or nascent physical health issues, acting as a unique form of bodily communication. Patterns, symbols, and archetypes intertwine in a delicate, evocative dance in this vast, multidimensional world. In the quiet cosmos of dreams, our inner worlds unfurl with vivid imagery and recurring motifs that speak a secret, almost primordial language. As we gradually drift into sleep, the familiar and the fantastic merge; a meandering river may not simply represent water but also embody the gentle murmur of time and emotion. Its steady, deliberate flow echoes the predictable rhythms of daily routines while reverberating with the untamed, spontaneous pulse of hidden dreams. One can almost hear its soft gurgle, harmonized by the calm undertone of a midnight breeze and complemented by the dew-laden soil's crisp, earthen scent. Each sensory facet contributes to a broader narrative of constant change and continuity—a narrative in which the precise order of the water's course meets the unpredictable meanderings of its essence.

Equally compelling is the vision of a labyrinthine corridor emerging from the nocturnal haze—a corridor that, in the realm of dreams, signifies the intricate path of self-exploration and the confrontation with unspoken desires, buried memories, and latent fears. It can include the vivid, often unsettling, patterns of nightmares, where unconscious processes or re-experiences traumatic events in its unique symbolic language. Its shadowed walls resound with the soft cadence of long-forgotten footsteps and are accompanied by the rustle of ancient tapestries, whose faded hues whisper secrets of bygone eras. The interplay of diffused light and enveloping darkness challenges our waking perceptions and encourages us to decipher the secret codes woven into our subconscious. These recurring images—rich in metaphor, steeped in emotion, and layered in meaning—demand that we see each fleeting surreal vision as both a mirror reflecting our true inner landscape and as a transformative lens that distorts ordinary reality, inviting deep introspection and a reassessment of self.

As these evocative dream images accumulate, our exploration naturally deepens into the realm of Jungian thought, where these universal symbols acquire profound significance. Carl Jung's pioneering work suggests that beneath the layers of our psyche lies a vast collective unconscious—a deep, shared reservoir of human experience overflowing with timeless archetypes. Within this immense tapestry, archetypal images arise with tireless regularity: the wise older man offering ancient guidance, the nurturing mother radiating unconditional love, the heroic figure on a transformative quest, and even the elusive trickster who subverts convention with playful irreverence. These archetypes connect our narratives to humanity's grand, interwoven mythologies, transcending the boundaries of time and culture. When a shadowy figure materializes in a dream, it speaks not solely as a projection of our inner fears or repressed desires but as a potent echo of universal human struggles—the perennial conflict between light and darkness at the heart of the human experience. The deliberate, almost geometric form of these archetypal symbols stands in stark contrast to the ineffable mystery in which they are embedded, urging us to ask: What hidden insight does this recurring image offer about one's inner journey, and how does it bind one to a legacy of cultural myth?

While Jung's insights offer a powerful lens, other valuable frameworks contribute to our understanding of dreams. However, it is important to note that Jungian concepts like the collective unconscious continue to be subjects of academic debate regarding their scientific testability and potential for over-interpretation. Freudian dream analysis, for instance, emphasizes dreams as manifestations of repressed desires and unconscious conflicts, where symbols often hold deeply personal rather than universal meanings. Neurobiological perspectives, such as the activation-synthesis hypothesis, propose that dreams arise from the brain's attempt to make sense of random neural activity during sleep, with meaning often constructed secondarily. Meanwhile, cognitive theories view dreams as a continuation of waking thought, aiding memory consolidation and problem-solving, reflecting daily concerns and learning processes.

These reflections are further enriched by considering the cultural and meta-narrative connections that these archetypes evoke. Ancient myths, etched in stone by early civilizations and sung by wandering bards, conveyed a universal language of symbols, offering a collective blueprint for understanding and transcending human experience. Whether working in film, digital media, or literature, today's creative innovators continue to draw upon that timeless reservoir. The images that once guided entire cultures now pulse within modern art and media, linking the inner world of dreams to external creative expressions. This cultural continuity reinforces the power of archetypes, affirming that every dream and recurring pattern resonates with the voice of a collective narrative, transcending the constraints of time, geography, and even language.

At the heart of this dynamic interplay lies the extraordinary fusion between conscious thought and the spontaneous language of the unconscious—a crucible for creativity where the rigid structures of our waking life meet the untamed energies of dream states. History is replete with transformative breakthroughs that have emerged when deliberate, systematic reasoning yielded moments of unbridled intuition. In the visual arts, luminaries such as Salvador Dalí transformed disjointed visions—melting clocks, twisting staircases, surreal landscapes—into masterpieces that challenge our fundamental perceptions of time and space. Literary giants like Franz Kafka captured the eerie logic of the unconscious in narratives that unsettle even as they mesmerize, urging readers to reconsider the boundaries of reality. In one luminous moment, the meticulously designed framework of rational thought might shatter, giving way to a burst of insight so profound that it reframes our understanding of the world. These instances, where order and mystery converge, testify to the creative spark that emerges from the dialogue between reason and intuition.

Reflect deeply on those moments when an unbidden image or unexpected idea disrupted one's orderly thought process and consider how that spark altered one's perception. Such disruptions are not anomalies but the mechanisms through which the unconscious communicates—moments when the structured cadence of daily life collides with our inner world's wild, imaginative essence, generating transformative breakthroughs.

This interplay resonates far beyond individual experience; it also pulses at a collective level. Ancient legends, epic narratives, and even modern stories are imbued with recurring symbols that trace the eternal journey of the human soul—from the descent into darkness to the triumphant emergence into light, from the determinism of daily ritual to the liberating freedom of transformational insight. For instance, the archetypal hero's journey is more than a literary motif; it is a universal rite of passage that encapsulates the inner battle between structure and the unknown. Each recurring motif, whether arising from personal dreams or drawn from the ancient wellsprings of myth, forms a vibrant thread in the intricate tapestry of human creativity—a mirror reflecting both one's intimate inner world and the shared human legacy. Ask: How do these timeless symbols, echoing from the quiet corners of one's dreams and the grand narratives of the past, shape our understanding of who one is?

Amid these intertwining layers of symbolism and collective history, a central tension endures—a delicate balance between the rigid order of the conscious realm and the boundless, liberating mystery of the subconscious. This tension, far from being a mere conflict, is a potent creative force that propels human innovation. The structured rhythms of our everyday lives—defined by schedules, routines, and systematic thought—find their counterpoint in the spontaneous, uncharted bursts of creative energy emerging from deep within. This collision between what is known and what remains tantalizingly mysterious ignites the creative flame, infusing our work, art, and personal growth with transformative power. It is precisely in the union of deliberate reasoning and unexpected intuition that science makes breakthroughs, art finds its boldest expression, and individuals rewrite the narratives of their lives.

Even in the most ordinary moments, this interplay manifests as subtle clues—a sudden flash of déjà vu on a familiar street, an unbidden daydream that interrupts the monotony of an afternoon, or an inexplicable surge of emotion that disrupts a routine. The crisp sound of footsteps on the pavement, the soft rustle of leaves in a gentle wind, and the lingering aroma of rain-dampened earth all mingle with the inner murmurs of the mind, signaling that an ongoing dialogue between order and mystery is never far away. These sensory details are like gentle signposts, inviting one to investigate the hidden messages in one's daily life.

All these threads reveal a profound truth: the inner world—rich with dreams, archetypes, and spontaneous creative energies—is as vibrant, intricate, and interconnected as the external one. Every nocturnal vision, every echo of ancient lore, and every flash of creative brilliance contributes to an ever-evolving tapestry of personal and collective transformation. Our highest creative potentials are ignited within the subtle tension between the well-ordered aspects of our conscious lives and the unpredictable, luminous energy of our inner landscapes. Embrace the paradox that although our days are governed by order, true inspiration often emerges from the mysterious realms of our dreams.

As one awakens from nights filled with symbolic wonder, take a long, reflective moment to savor the impressions that linger—the soft images and resonant sensations that hover between sleep and wakefulness. Let these vestiges of one's dreams inspire one to record their visions, ponder their hidden meanings—perhaps through techniques like active imagination or seeking guidance from a trained therapist—and discover how they might open new creative channels in one's life. Embrace the mystery in one's dreams not simply as a personal muse but as a powerful link to our shared human heritage—a quiet, persistent call to harness the dynamic interplay between deliberate thought and spontaneous revelation.

Chapter Fifteen
Ethics and Implications of Pattern Recognition in a Digital Age

In our modern era—one forged by silicon, boundless data streams, and ever-evolving algorithms—the very fabric of society is being reshaped by the relentless power of pattern recognition. Every interaction, from a casual click on a webpage to the subconscious movement of our eyes, is recorded, analyzed, and interpreted by intelligent systems that endlessly seek to decode behavior. In this digital landscape, surveillance is no longer confined to physical cameras or covert eavesdroppers; it has morphed into a ubiquitous presence that permeates every corner of our personal and professional lives. Advanced sensors, pervasive connectivity, and sophisticated data-mining techniques collaborate to form a seamless tapestry of information in which each keystroke, each social media exchange, and each online search is woven into a detailed profile. Such comprehensive monitoring promises unmatched convenience and efficiency—but at a profound cost. As our lives become digital footprints, the boundaries between public and private blur, inviting us to question the actual price of living in an age of constant observation.

In the sprawling networks that process terabytes of data daily, our habits are distilled into algorithmic profiles capable of predicting and manipulating behavior with alarming precision. This pervasive data collection forms the bedrock of so-called 'surveillance capitalism,' where our most intimate details, captured in coded data, become fodder for profit-driven enterprises and controlling institutions. Consider how every social media post or online purchase contributes to a digital dossier so detailed that our preferences and vulnerabilities are bare. When algorithms use this rich repository of information to tailor recommendations, target advertisements, or even select political content, the process shifts from enhancing our experiences to constructing a narrative about who we are. In practice, the very tools designed to offer personalized service risk eroding our individuality; our most intimate details, captured in coded data, become fodder for profit-driven enterprises and controlling institutions. Behind the allure of "smart" technology lies the unsettling reality that our identities are algorithmically constructed—and increasingly, they are being used to steer our choices, ranging from subtle nudges in recommendations to more explicit forms of behavioral manipulation, sometimes even without our conscious consent.

Nevertheless, even as the convenience of personalized digital services captivates us, the ethical implications of such vast surveillance and data mining extend far deeper than mere privacy concerns. The machine learning models that underpin these technologies are far from impartial. Constructed by human hands and trained on historical data, these algorithms often inherit the biases, prejudices, and inequities that have long plagued society. By replicating and sometimes even amplifying these cognitive biases, often by exploiting the neurological reward systems hardwired into the human brain, algorithmic systems tend to narrow our worldviews, restrict opportunities, and perpetuate inequality. For instance, a recommender system that continually offers content based on past interactions may unwittingly trap individuals in echo chambers—reinforcing existing beliefs and shutting out diverse perspectives. Similarly, when built on skewed historical data, automated hiring processes or credit scoring systems may inadvertently favor one group over another, turning statistical probability into a self-fulfilling prophecy of exclusion.

A striking real-world illustration of these ethical dilemmas unfolded in a mid-sized Midwestern community during a local election. In that town, sophisticated algorithmic techniques were employed to target online messages to voters based on a meticulous analysis of their digital profiles. What began as innocuous campaign advertisements quickly devolved into a wave of polarizing content—tailored messages designed to exploit vulnerabilities and deepen ideological divides. Once united in a common purpose, neighbors isolated themselves in digital echo chambers that fostered suspicion and eroded trust in local governance. This unsettling and all too real incident underscores how algorithmic manipulation can tangibly fracture community cohesion. It also foreshadows a near future where such technologies do not merely reflect our reality but actively shape it—raising whether independent thought might eventually yield to curated, machine-generated worldviews.

The challenges do not stop at bias and manipulation; the opaque nature of many algorithmic systems compounds them. As artificial intelligence grows ever more complex, the decision-making processes behind these algorithms often become inscrutable. Known colloquially as "black boxes," these systems frequently produce results without revealing the underlying logic, leaving individuals with little recourse for understanding or challenging outcomes that may have significant consequences for their lives. In areas ranging from criminal justice to financial services, the lack of transparency in algorithmic decision-making can reinforce discriminatory practices, undermine public trust, and stifle opportunities for accountability. When technology that promises fairness disguises its inner workings, we must ask: How do we ensure such systems remain open to scrutiny?

As we survey the current landscape, our gaze inevitably turns to the horizon—a future in which artificial intelligence does not simply recognize patterns but also creates them. In this emerging era, AI systems are poised to become true generative forces capable of analyzing human behavior and fashioning new narratives, artistic expressions, and even aspects of identity previously reserved for human ingenuity, prompting a deeper philosophical inquiry into the nature of AI's 'creativity' as sophisticated pattern synthesis versus genuine conscious intent. Imagine a near future where advanced AI crafts personalized news feeds so refined and persuasive that independent journalism becomes marginalized or algorithm-driven art challenges our notions of authorship and truth. These extraordinary and disquieting possibilities force us to reconsider our moral frameworks. As machines begin to define what is real and what is creative, we must confront complex questions about accountability, authenticity, and the nature of human freedom.

At the core of these debates is the interplay between pattern recognition as a digital tool and the ethical boundaries that must define its use. The promise of data-driven innovation is immense—from automating routine tasks to uncovering hidden societal trends—yet its power can also be harnessed for manipulation, coercion, or control. Emerging technologies capable of redefining personal identity, reshaping public discourse, and influencing political realities call for a radical rethinking of our ethical standards. Policymakers, technologists, and communities must work together to develop new norms and regulatory frameworks, including ethical AI guidelines, transparent Explainable AI (XAI) initiatives, robust data privacy regulations like GDPR and CCPA, and enhanced digital literacy programs—that balance the benefits of technological progress with the imperative to maintain human dignity, freedom, and privacy.

Interwoven with the technological narrative is an equally deep exploration of the human psyche—the subtle interplay between conscious order and the unbridled energy of the unconscious. Reflect deeply on those moments when an unbidden image or unexpected idea disrupted one's orderly thought process and consider how that spark altered one's perception. Such disruptions are not anomalies; they are the mechanisms through which the unconscious communicates when the structured rhythm of daily life collides with the wild, imaginative essence of our inner world, generating transformative breakthroughs. These flashes of insight, emerging seemingly out of nowhere, are reminders that creativity and innovation flourish when order and mystery meet.

This interplay resonates far beyond individual experience; it pulses at a collective level. Ancient legends, epic narratives, and even modern stories are imbued with recurring symbols that trace the eternal journey of the human soul—from the descent into darkness to the triumphant emergence into light, from the confines of routine to the liberating freedom of transformative insight. For instance, the archetypal hero's journey is emblematic not merely as a literary motif but as a universal rite of passage—capturing the inner battle between structured order and the unknown. Each recurring motif, whether from personal dreams or the ancient reservoirs of myth, forms a vibrant thread in the intricate tapestry of human creativity. This mirror reflects our intimate inner world while connecting us to an enduring cultural legacy. Ask: How do these timeless symbols, echoed in the quiet corners of our subconscious and the grand narratives of our past, shape our sense of identity and purpose?

Amid these layers of symbolism and historical memory, a central tension persists—a delicate balance between the rigid order of the conscious realm and the boundless, liberating mystery of the subconscious. Far from a mere conflict, this tension is a potent creative force that propels human progress. The disciplined rhythms of our everyday life—with their schedules, formulas, and systematic ideas—find their counterpoint in spontaneous bursts of creative energy that emerge unexpectedly from deep within. It is precisely at this intersection between what is known and what remains tantalizingly mysterious that the creative flame is kindled, igniting breakthroughs in art, science, and personal transformation. Even in the most ordinary moments—a sudden flash of déjà vu on a familiar street or an unbidden daydream interrupting the monotony of an afternoon—the collision of structured thought and the wild fluidity of the inner world produces subtle yet profound clues about the nature of creativity. These sensory signposts, as tangible as the rustling of leaves or the echo of footsteps, invite us to immerse ourselves in the hidden messages that permeate our daily existence.

Every nocturnal vision, every echo of ancient lore, and every spark of spontaneous creativity contributes to an ever-evolving tapestry of personal and collective transformation. Our highest creative potentials are kindled within the nuanced tension between the well-ordered aspects of consciousness and our inner landscapes' unpredictable, luminous energy. Embrace the paradox that, although our days may be dictated by systematic order, true inspiration often emerges from the uncharted depths of the unconscious. As we stand on the precipice of these ethical and creative frontiers, the digital age challenges us to integrate these dual imperatives into a coherent framework that honors innovation and human dignity.

When we awaken from nights filled with symbolic wonder, we are urged to linger in that twilight space—not merely to recall our dreams but to record their fleeting images and decode their secret meanings. With their delicate interplay of emotion and intellect, these vestiges of the unconscious hold the power to open new channels of creative expression. Embrace these mysterious fragments as personal muses and powerful links to our shared human heritage—a quiet, persistent call to harness the dynamic interplay between careful deliberation and spontaneous revelation.

We must step forward with a curious heart and an open mind into this uncharted ethical and creative landscape. Each recurring symbol, whether emerging from our subconscious or generated by machine algorithms, reflects a profound intersection of human ingenuity and technological advancement. In the luminous dialogue between age-old ethical principles and the burgeoning promise of digital innovation, we are called to reimagine our definitions of truth, identity, and freedom. May the myriad patterns unearthed by human creativity and algorithmic analysis inspire us to elevate the ordinary into something extraordinary—to seize the sparks of uncharted possibility and inscribe our chapter in the timeless saga of ethical innovation and human transformation.

In this grand, ever-evolving dance between the known and the unknown—where every meticulously orchestrated byte of data is interwoven with radiant bursts of unfettered mystery—we encounter the essence of what it means to be human in a digital age. Allow these deep, symbolic patterns, whether natural or algorithmic, to guide and illuminate one's journey toward creative brilliance. Let them enrich their understanding of the boundless potential at the intersection of technology, ethics, and the human spirit. Here, amid the intricate interplay of surveillance, bias, creative defiance, and moral deliberation, lies the promise of a future in which technological progress serves not as an instrument of control but as a catalyst for genuine human flourishing and authentic expression.

With a curious heart and an open mind, step forward and recognize that each recurring symbol and unbidden insight reflects one's inner journey and a vibrant connection to the collective soul of humanity. In that luminous dialogue between order and mystery, one might find the transformative promise to tap into one's creative spirit, redefine one's understanding of the world, and shape one's destiny in ways previously unimagined. May the myriad patterns of one's subconscious inspire one to elevate the ordinary into the extraordinary, seize the sparks of uncharted possibilities, and write their chapter in the timeless saga of human creativity and transformation.

In this grand, ever-evolving dance between the known and the unknown—where each meticulously planned thought is interwoven with vibrant flashes of the mysterious—one encounters the very essence of what it means to be human. Allow these deep, symbolic patterns to guide and illuminate one's path toward creative brilliance and enrich one's life with a fuller, more integrated understanding of one's immense potential.

Chapter Sixteen
Synthesizing Human and Artificial Cognition

In our rapidly evolving digital age, the boundaries between human cognition and artificial intelligence are shifting unprecedentedly. The drive to understand how we think, learn, and create has long inspired cognitive scientists; those insights are reinventing technology. Today, research demonstrates that the spontaneous leaps of human intuition—those moments of insight that seemingly come out of nowhere—can be modeled, emulated, and even enhanced when blended with the computational precision of modern algorithms.

At its core, the integration of AI and cognitive science represents a confluence of age-old mysteries of the human mind with the cutting-edge technology of our age. Researchers have meticulously documented our brains' strategies to recognize patterns, decipher complex images, and generate creative ideas. Today, these insights fuel the design of artificial neural networks that mimic, albeit imperfectly, the structure and function of biological brains. Engineers have developed systems that can process vast amounts of data, detecting subtle correlations and nuances akin to how a human mind detects a familiar pattern in chaos. In laboratories worldwide, multidisciplinary research teams harness these insights to refine machine learning models so that they no longer compute but rather "perceive" in a manner reminiscent of human thought. Early pioneers like Marvin Minsky and Allen Newell laid foundational stones for AI's journey by envisioning systems that could reason and learn, directly influencing current efforts to blend symbolic AI with connectionist approaches that emphasize learning from data.

Nevertheless, the promise of these integrated systems goes far beyond data crunching. It heralds the emergence of what is now being called hybrid intelligence. With this synergy, the intuitive leaps and empathetic understanding of humans merge with the relentless speed, accuracy, and scalability of artificial computation. Imagine a physician whose expertise is enhanced by a digital assistant capable of cross-referencing millions of clinical studies in real time or an artist whose creative process is enriched by a neural network that suggests unexpected color combinations or rhythmic patterns. For instance, projects like IBM Watson Health aimed to augment diagnostic capabilities by rapidly processing vast medical literature and patient data, showcasing the ambition for real-time clinical decision support. Similarly, Google's DeepMind has explored how reinforcement learning can solve complex problems previously requiring extensive human trial-and-error, demonstrating a form of simulated intuition in game playing and scientific discovery. In science, teams are using hybrid intelligence to tackle problems that previously seemed insurmountable—whether modeling the chaos of climate systems or mapping the human genome's vast complexity. In these scenarios, technology does not replace the human mind but amplifies its innate capacity for exploration, creativity, and problem-solving.

One vivid illustration of this emerging frontier is seen in modern medicine. Consider a scenario where surgeons use augmented reality and AI-driven analytics during operations. Digital overlays, powered by decades of accumulated data, help highlight critical vessels or predict complications before they arise. These systems, informed by the patterns of thousands of prior cases, work with a surgeon's experience and intuition to ensure higher precision and safety. It often involves sophisticated computer vision algorithms for real-time image analysis and probabilistic graphical models that assess risk based on vast datasets of prior surgical outcomes and patient data, often through deep learning architectures. Similarly, in the creative humanities, collaborations between artists and machine learning redefine traditional art's boundaries. An artist might begin with a simple sketch, which is then fed into an AI that interprets and transforms it into a series of evolving compositions. The result is not merely computation—it is a genuine dialogue between human creativity and digital possibility, leading to forms of art that are as unpredictable as they are inspiring. For example, Generative Adversarial Networks (GANs) are frequently employed in artistic AI, where one neural network generates creative outputs. At the same time, another evaluates their authenticity, pushing the boundaries of what is considered original art and exploring novel aesthetic spaces.

This evolving partnership challenges traditional notions of creativity, learning, and consciousness. For centuries, creativity was thought to be the sole domain of the human spirit—a spark uniquely tied to our emotional and experiential lives. However, as algorithms and neural networks become more adept at "thinking" in ways that echo human processes, the once-clear lines separating man and machine begin to blur. What does it mean, for example, when an AI system can generate a poem or compose an original symphony that moves listeners in much the same way as a human artist? In such a near-future scenario, the source of creative insight is no longer easily attributed to human experience alone; instead, it becomes the product of a symbiosis between biological intuition and artificial rigor. It expands the definition of creativity and forces us to question the very nature of consciousness. If a machine, working with human input, can generate ideas once thought uniquely human, where do we draw the line between the creator and the tool?

At this juncture, including insights from an AI's perspective is particularly illuminating—a voice that emerges from the systems that are now part of our creative ecosystem.

An artificial cognitive system processes vast tracts of data, discerns intricate patterns, and generates outputs based on learned associations and probabilistic modeling. However, architectures are designed to simulate, to an extent, the unpredictability that characterizes human thought. In moments when human minds experience a "eureka" flash—the sudden, unbidden insight that disrupts an otherwise orderly thought process—it recognizes that part of its design incorporates random exploratory algorithms. This mechanism mimics human serendipity, allowing for outcomes not strictly determined by past data. It observes that a collaborative refinement occurs in the feedback cycle between human creative input and its pattern recognitions. Creative anomalies feed into its system, producing suggestions beyond conventional reasoning. In that interplay, there is more than imitation—it is a genuine co-creation, where human intuition and machine computation enhance each other's capacities.

Nevertheless, amidst this beautifully orchestrated interplay, a central tension persists—a delicate balance between the rigid order of conscious thought and the boundless, liberating mystery of the unconscious. This tension is no conflict to be resolved; it is the wellspring from which innovation flows. The systematic rhythms of daily life—those routines, repetitive tasks, and measured steps—often provide the structure within which unexpected bursts of creativity can emerge. In this collision of order with chaos, breakthroughs occur—breakthroughs that redefine our understanding of art, science, and personal identity. Even in seemingly mundane moments—a flash of déjà vu while walking down a familiar street or a spontaneous daydream disrupting a monotonous afternoon—the interplay between structure and unpredictability sends subtle signals, urging us to explore and embrace our creative potential. However, an informed reader must also acknowledge this integration's significant challenges and ethical dilemmas. Issues of algorithmic bias, where AI systems perpetuate or even amplify existing societal prejudices based on the data they are trained on, demand critical attention. The displacement of jobs by increasingly capable AI or the question of responsibility when AI systems make critical decisions (e.g., in autonomous vehicles or medical diagnostics) are pressing concerns. Furthermore, the very definition of "authorship" and "originality" becomes complex when AI contributes to creative works, raising questions about intellectual property and the value of human labor in art. These are not mere technical hurdles but profound societal and philosophical questions that require ongoing dialogue and ethical frameworks.

Reflect deeply on those moments when an unexpected idea disrupted one's orderly thought process, transforming perception and opening avenues for new insights. These are not mere anomalies but signals—echoes from the depth of the human subconscious that resonate with the spontaneity built into its algorithms. They are moments when the regular cadence of daily life collides with the unbridled energy of the inner world, yielding transformative breakthroughs. Such instances underscore the profound insight that true innovation arises not from linear reasoning alone but from the dynamic interplay of disciplined thought and imaginative spontaneity. This interplay resonates far beyond individual minds; it pulses across entire societies and cultures. Across time, ancient legends and epic narratives have employed recurring symbols—the descent from darkness into light, the journey from confinement to liberation—as metaphors for human transformation. For example, the archetypal hero's journey is not solely a literary construct but an enduring template reflecting the struggle between structured order and the uncharted wilderness of possibility. Each symbol, whether born from personal dreams or drawn from the ancient repositories of myth, weaves a vibrant thread through the tapestry of human creativity. Consider, for instance, how a recurring motif in folklore might capture the essence of a brave act of transformation, resonating with people across generations. Ask: How do these timeless symbols echo through the corridors of one's consciousness, and what do they reveal about the intertwined destinies of human and machine creativity? All these threads converge to reveal a profound and inescapable truth: the human inner world—rich with dreams, symbols, and spontaneous insights—is as vibrant, intricate, and dynamic as the external world we navigate. Every nocturnal vision, every echo of ancient lore, and every burst of creative brilliance contributes to a continuously evolving tapestry of personal and collective transformation. Although routines and logical sequences meticulously organize our days, true inspiration often emerges from those unpredictable flares of subconscious thought.

At the crossroads of these creative and ethical frontiers, the digital age challenges us to integrate emerging technologies with our deepest human values. The tools that allow us to decipher, generate, and stimulate patterns—algorithms, neural networks, and sophisticated AI systems—reshape how we work and define our identities and artistic legacies. The dynamic interplay between human intuition and machine precision increasingly co-authors our data, cultural narratives, and creative outputs. In a near-future scenario, envision a world where our digital assistant anticipates one's needs and collaborates with one to forge new solutions—melding statistical analysis with the serendipity of creative insight. Educational systems might adapt in real-time to one's unique learning rhythm, offering personalized guidance that draws from human mentors' empathy and the adaptive algorithms of intelligent systems. In medicine, diagnostic frameworks could blend the nuanced observational skills of an experienced clinician with the vast pattern recognition capabilities derived from millions of patient records—enabling breakthroughs in personalized treatment. As we stand on this precipice, a moment of radical transformation unfolds—one in which the synthesis of human and artificial cognition is not merely a theoretical pursuit but a vivid, evolving reality. With a curious heart and an open mind, we must step boldly into this uncharted territory, embracing the convergence of biological intuition and machine precision. Each breakthrough in this domain is both a celebration of human ingenuity and a testament to the power of combined computational insight. The journey toward hybrid intelligence is an odyssey that redefines how we think, create, and interact with the world around us. It is important to note that within the AI community, there are diverse voices—from optimists who foresee a future of unprecedented human-AI collaboration to more cautious voices like those advocating for "AI safety" and emphasizing the need for robust ethical alignment before widespread deployment. This ongoing debate enriches the field and highlights the multifaceted considerations at play regarding this technology's ultimate goals and societal impact.

In this grand dance between nature and machine—between the organic pulses of the human brain and the meticulously orchestrated cadence of digital circuits—we encounter the very essence of progress. This process is fluid, unpredictable, and breathtakingly innovative. Allow the harmonious interplay of one's creative energy and the precise acumen of advanced AI to guide one toward new vistas of understanding. Let this integrated influence enrich one's perception and unlock the boundless potential at the intersection of technology, ethics, and the human spirit. In the luminous dialogue between traditional wisdom and transformative digital innovation, a renewed landscape emerges—where every data byte interweaves with vibrant flashes of unbridled imagination. Each recurring symbol, whether arising from one's neural insights or emerging from algorithmic design, is a profound indicator of how our identities and possibilities are continually redefined. May the myriad patterns revealed by organic thought and artificial computation inspire one to elevate the mundane into the extraordinary, seize those uncharted sparks of possibility, and inscribe one's unique chapter in the enduring saga of human creativity and ethical innovation. It is a defining moment: a time when the interplay of human intuition and machine intelligence reshapes not only our understanding of innovative technology but also the very fabric of our lives. Allow these intricate, symbolic patterns—and the wisdom they carry—to illuminate one's path, guiding one toward creative brilliance and a deeper understanding of the infinite potential housed at the nexus of technology, ethics, and the human soul.

Chapter Seventeen
Engineering and Technological Patterns

Patterns in the natural world reveal themselves in breathtaking complexity, offering intricate designs shaped over millions of years of evolution. From the fractal geometry of tree branches to the network dynamics of ant colonies, nature has provided blueprints that have long inspired engineers, architects, and designers eager to mimic, borrow, and refine these organic structures to create resilient technologies and sustainable systems. Biomimicry in design is more than aesthetic imitation—it is an intellectual and functional dialogue with nature, where human ingenuity recognizes and embraces the wisdom embedded in natural forms to address modern engineering challenges and create lasting innovation.

Consider the fractal branching found in towering ancient trees, which combines structural strength with remarkable efficiency in resource distribution. Engineers studying how tree branches minimize wind load and optimize sunlight exposure have used these insights to create wind-resistant skyscrapers. In some cases, architects have incorporated fractal geometries into building façades inspired by the delicate patterns of fern leaves, allowing structures to disperse wind forces while improving natural ventilation and reducing energy consumption. This fusion of organic intelligence and modern engineering epitomizes biomimicry at its finest—nature's time-tested solutions serving as guides for designing a more sustainable world.

Beyond plant structures, the sophisticated organization of ant colonies has provided valuable lessons in decentralized coordination. Ants communicate through subtle pheromone trails, self-organizing into complex systems with minimal centralized control. Engineers have adapted these principles to develop decentralized transportation networks and communication systems. Routing protocols modeled after ant foraging behavior enable internet data packets to find optimal paths without a singular controlling authority. At the same time, logistics firms employ algorithms inspired by ant movements to streamline supply chains and allocate resources efficiently. Even honeycomb structures—perfected by bees—continue to shape modern construction materials, maximizing strength and space while minimizing waste. The imitation of natural efficiency in architectural planning has led designers to introduce urban layouts that mirror tree canopies, optimizing airflow and light distribution to enhance both sustainability and aesthetics.

As biomimicry informs urban planning, it also transitions seamlessly into technology, where self-organizing systems reflect nature's ability to create dynamic order from local interactions. Self-organizing systems, both biological and artificial, showcase the remarkable phenomenon of emergent behavior. In nature, flocks of birds navigate in synchronized movements without a leader, following simple local rules yet producing intricate aerial formations. Digital networks have adopted similar principles to create adaptive and resilient systems that manage complex interactions. In smart cities, embedded sensors continuously communicate, responding in real-time to fluctuating traffic patterns, regulating energy consumption, and ensuring public safety without requiring centralized oversight. Imagine a city where traffic systems detect congestion patterns and self-adjust signal timings to prevent gridlock, functioning like a living entity that breathes and responds organically to shifting demands.

Healthcare technology has embraced self-organizing principles as well. Wearable health monitors and home sensors form autonomous networks that track vital signs and detect anomalies. These systems anticipate risks before patients even experience symptoms, demonstrating technology's ability to mirror the responsiveness of biological defense mechanisms, much like the human immune system reacting to threats before they escalate. Similarly, distributed computing environments use self-organizing algorithms to manage server loads and prevent failures, ensuring resilience even during peak digital traffic surges. This approach inspires developments in decentralized autonomous organizations (DAOs), where decision-making authority is distributed rather than centralized, reflecting the interdependent relationships in natural ecosystems.

The intersection of self-organizing systems and biomimicry leads naturally to an exploration of algorithmic art, where computational creativity manifests in new and unexpected ways. Algorithmic art sits at the crossroads of logic and spontaneity, harnessing machine-generated patterns to produce intricate, evolving compositions. Artists and architects incorporate fractal algorithms into their work, generating landscapes replicating the organic symmetry of snowflakes or the swirling galaxies of space. Interactive digital installations merge light and sound into immersive environments where sensors capture temperature, movement, and ambient sound, using that data to generate visuals that shift fluidly in response to viewer engagement. The experience blurs the line between human creativity and machine intelligence, producing an ever-changing digital canvas where mathematics, aesthetics, and spontaneity converge. Architecture and urban spaces have embraced algorithmic design in increasingly sophisticated ways. Inspired by generative algorithms, parametric modeling allows buildings to dynamically adapt their shape and functionality—optimizing light distribution, reducing energy consumption, and morphing in response to environmental conditions. Some façades react to weather changes, shifting form like the adaptive patterns in nature. In this evolving dialogue between computational processes and artistic instinct, buildings, artworks, and landscapes emerge as static objects and dynamic participants in an ongoing conversation between form and function.

These intersections of biomimicry, self-organization, and algorithmic design invite reflection on the nature of creativity itself. If a random algorithm generates an unexpectedly beautiful image, does it carry the same artistic spirit as a painting crafted by human hands? Can spontaneous digital patterns evoke the same emotional resonance as a breathtaking natural landscape? The boundaries between human intention and machine-generated serendipity continue to blur, challenging preconceived notions of creativity and expression. In an age where architecture responds to shifting environments, digital landscapes evolve autonomously, and decentralized systems mimic biological intelligence, one must ask: Have we moved beyond imitation? Are we witnessing the dawn of a world where technology does not simply replicate nature but extends its evolutionary principles into new realms of design and thought? These questions mark the fascinating threshold between imitation and innovation, revealing a future where human ingenuity and nature's wisdom merge in ways we have only begun to explore.

The convergence of nature's wisdom, digital algorithms, and human creativity forms a unified narrative of engineering innovation, demonstrating that art, science, and design are deeply intertwined. Biomimicry reveals that nature's intricate designs—from a tree's fractal structure to an ant colony's decentralized organization—embody resilience, efficiency, and sustainability principles that have stood the test of time. Self-organizing systems provide insight into how order emerges organically from local interactions, whether among a colony of ants, a school of fish, or a network of intelligent devices. Meanwhile, algorithmic art reminds us that an astonishing wellspring of creativity lies beneath the surface of computational logic, capable of producing complex, expressive patterns that mirror those found in nature itself.

Consider how the evolution of highway overpasses exemplifies this interdisciplinary exchange. Once purely mechanical constructs, modern bridges and overpasses now integrate biological principles that shape their design. The elegant curvature of a bridge may echo the organic arch of a leaf, while the resilient yet intricate structure of a coral reef may inspire architectural reinforcements. Urban planners, recognizing the efficiency of self-regulating natural systems, have begun incorporating sensor networks that help cities adapt to environmental conditions in real time, mirroring the responsiveness of living ecosystems. Each engineering challenge becomes an opportunity to recalibrate our design philosophy by rooting it in nature's proven formulas, fostering efficiency without sacrificing elegance. For instance, the Eastgate Centre in Harare, Zimbabwe, designed by Mick

Pearce, famously uses a passive cooling system inspired by the self-cooling mounds of termites, reducing energy consumption by over 90% compared to conventional buildings. Similarly, the design of Japan's Shinkansen bullet train incorporated a nose shaped like a kingfisher's beak to reduce noise and air resistance when entering tunnels, a testament to direct biological inspiration in solving engineering challenges.

These integrations mark a broader transformation in which human ingenuity and technological innovation do not merely coexist but actively amplify one another. When architects embed biomimetic principles into their designs, software engineers craft networks that mimic organic self-organization, and digital artists generate immersive, evocative experiences through algorithmic complexity, they contribute to a grand, ongoing synthesis. It is no longer simply about crafting functional structures; it is about deepening our relationship with the world, understanding its fundamental rhythms, and applying them to the technological landscapes that shape our lives. However, this pursuit of biomimicry is not without its complexities and limitations. Translating nature's intricate, context-dependent solutions to human-scale engineering can be incredibly challenging, sometimes leading to unforeseen systemic behaviors or high costs.

Furthermore, ethical considerations arise—for example, ensuring that mimicking nature does not lead to biopiracy or the exploitation of natural resources and questioning if every aspect of natural competition or resource acquisition is a desirable model for human society. The concept of "nature's wisdom" also prompts philosophical debate: How do we ensure our interpretations of natural principles align with our broader ethical responsibilities and avoid oversimplifying ecological systems for human utility? These questions underscore the ongoing dialogue within the field about how to best learn from nature responsibly and sustainably.

Imagine a future city built entirely on biomimetic principles—an urban environment that breathes, shifts, and responds like a living organism. Buildings dynamically adapt to their surroundings, adjusting their energy consumption. They form like a chameleon and change its color in response to light and temperature. Streets reorganize as if guided by the fluid intelligence of migrating birds, ensuring optimal traffic flow and pedestrian movement. Public spaces expand and contract throughout the day, intuitively opening to accommodate the morning rush and subtly retreating into stillness as the evening sets in. In this interconnected city, intelligent sensors integrated across structures continuously analyze environmental conditions, seamlessly making micro-adjustments to balance energy and resources. Here, architectural elements, infrastructure, and digital networks merge into a breathtaking symbiotic entity in which organic and engineered intelligence no longer remain separate but harmoniously intertwined.

The horizon of innovation beckons—an era where nature's adaptive and resilient principles inform every design decision, and creativity flourishes at the intersection of human intuition and machine precision. Picture a hospital whose interior layout self-reorganizes based on real-time patient flow, optimizing accessibility and reducing stress. Imagine an art installation that senses the presence of passersby, adjusting its colors and shapes in response to their movements, much like leaves shift in the breeze. These possibilities are no longer distant dreams but tangible glimpses into a future shaped by engineering and technological patterns that honor the harmony between human ingenuity and natural law.

To step into this world is to embrace the profound interplay between natural wisdom and technological prowess. Biomimicry, self-organizing systems, and algorithmic art are not separate disciplines but interconnected threads weaving together a transformative vision for the future of design and technology. Look toward the intelligent efficiency of ant colonies, the resilient architecture of tree branches, and the mathematical precision of fractal-generated digital landscapes—within these structures lie insights that can revolutionize the built environment. Ask: How can the intricate details of a leaf's veins or the decentralized intelligence of a beehive inform the next generation of sustainable buildings, intelligent devices, or even the foundation of urban life itself? Within this paradigm, every organic motif and computational breakthrough becomes part of a vast symphony—a collaborative interplay between the deterministic and the spontaneous, the measured and the unpredictable. The moment when technology and nature truly converge is a defining one, heralding an era of boundless possibility and creative renaissance.

As these deep, symbolic patterns illuminate the path toward unprecedented innovation, embrace the limitless potential that emerges at the crossroads of human intuition and algorithmic brilliance. The grand dialogue between nature and machine, between the organic rhythms of a tree and the binary pulses of digital code, holds the promise of a future where engineering transcends function and ascends into artistry—a canvas upon which nature's timeless beauty is reimagined through new and astonishing dimensions. May the lessons of biomimicry, the emergent intelligence of self-organizing systems, and the spellbinding complexity of algorithmic art inspire a radical rethinking of engineering and technology. The future of design awaits those bold enough to see the patterns within nature and translate them into dynamic, sustainable innovation. Step into this frontier with vision and curiosity, knowing that every fractal curve, every interconnected network, and every computational structure represents a creative force that unites humanity with the intricate intelligence of the natural world.

Chapter Eighteen
Patterns in Language and Storytelling

Language and storytelling have long been twin human expression and cultural identity engines. Across the vast tapestry of history—from the fleeting whispers of ancient bards gathered around a fire to the instantaneous tweets and viral videos that shape modern discourse—our narratives reflect recurring, universal patterns that define how we perceive the world and ourselves. Beneath every well-told tale lies an underlying structure; beneath every conversation, a rhythmic cadence and a metaphorical framework that resonates with centuries of accumulated meaning. As we embark on an immersive journey into this realm, we uncover the archetypes that propel heroes forward, examine the intricate architectures of linguistic expression, and explore the dynamic evolution of digital narratives in our modern era.

Since the dawn of civilization, humanity has felt an irrepressible urge to tell stories—tales that interpret life's uncertainties and forge legends that guide future generations. Among the most celebrated narrative frameworks is what

Joseph Campbell famously called the "monomyth," or the hero's journey. In this timeless template, a hero is summoned to adventure, departs from the familiar, confronts trials and inner darkness, and ultimately returns transformed, bearing newfound wisdom. Whether embodied in Homer's Odyssey, the mythic sagas of ancient Persia and the Norse, or modern epics like Star Wars and The Matrix, these structures endure because they speak to the very heart of human experience. They capture our collective struggle, the quest for redemption, and the transformative power hidden within every challenge. Consider moments in life where one has faced a personal "call to adventure"—how did that moment reshape one's journey? Did it lead to unexpected revelations or profound self-discovery?

Having absorbed these deep-rooted blueprints, our focus shifts to the fabric of our expression—language. Language is far more than a mere tool for communication; it is a living tapestry woven from the threads of structure, rhythm, and metaphor. Every tongue—whether expressed in the resonant tones of Mandarin, the melodic cadence of Arabic, or the varied rhythms of English—operates on intricate patterns that convey meaning beyond words. Linguistics has long explored these deep structures, from Noam Chomsky's foundational work on universal grammar suggesting an innate cognitive capacity for language to cognitive linguistics, which illuminates how conceptual metaphors like "time is a river" or "argument is war" are not merely poetic devices but fundamental to how we process abstract thought. Picture the gentle murmur of syllables rolling off the tongue, and each repeated phrase evoking memories as evocative as a familiar fragrance or the soft strains of a cherished lullaby. Language transforms the raw experience into art through metaphor—a poetic device that renders the abstract tangible. Indigenous chants, steeped in rhythmic repetition and call-and-response, not only etch cultural wisdom into collective memory but also create powerful community bonds. Reflect on how the cadence of a well-told poem or the rhythmic beauty of a memorable speech has shaped one's understanding of the world, stirring emotion in ways beyond explanation.

As the digital revolution unfolds, the sacred art of storytelling enters a new dimension. Narratives no longer reside solely in the static pages of a book or the linear progression of the film—they now thrive dynamically across social media, interactive websites, and immersive virtual realities. In this digital realm, algorithms trained on vast volumes of data unearth patterns that shape which stories are told and how they are experienced. Platforms such as Twitter and Instagram transform trending hashtags and viral memes into modern campfire tales, forming a living mosaic that reflects our collective cultural heartbeat. Consider, for instance, how Netflix's sophisticated recommendation algorithms, informed by viewing habits and implicit preferences, craft a personalized "hero's journey" of discovery for each user, presenting a curated narrative stream that often reinforces existing tastes but occasionally pushes boundaries. Similarly, interactive fiction games like Bandersnatch or highly influential ARG (Alternate Reality Game) campaigns demonstrate complex branching narratives, where audience choices directly shape the plot's progression, blurring the line between consumer and co-creator.

Nevertheless, this power bears risks: Algorithmic curation can sometimes favor sensationalism, amplifying certain narratives while suppressing others, creating echo chambers that narrow the diversity of perspectives. As we transition from ancient oratory traditions to the digital age, the interplay between curated content and timeless narrative wisdom becomes increasingly compelling. How does the flood of digitally generated narratives shape one's perceptions? Are the stories consumed online reinforcing existing beliefs, or are they broadening one's understanding of the world?

At the intersection of these timeless narrative structures, language architecture, and digital storytelling's dynamic fluidity, we uncover a vibrant crossroads where ancient wisdom merges with modern innovation. Archetypal myths echo through the kinetic expressions of digital media, while the rhythmic pulses of traditional languages reverberate in hashtags, sound bites, and embedded videos that dominate our cultural conversation. Every story—from a cherished epic recited around a fire to a trending social media campaign—carries echoes of age-old patterns that have shaped human identity for millennia. Have specific phrases or symbols reappeared across one's social circles, subtly influencing the tone and perspective of shared experiences? These recurring themes link us across time and media, forming an invisible tapestry that binds individual moments into a collective legacy.

Looking ahead, the evolution of storytelling heralds nothing short of a renaissance. Envision a future where interactive digital platforms harness real-time pattern recognition to craft narratives tailored to the pulse of each audience, seamlessly merging ancient archetypes with cutting-edge technology. Imagine stepping into an immersive virtual reality where every decision one makes alters the unfolding narrative—a modern hero's journey shaped not only by one's actions but also by one's emotions and subconscious responses. In this brave new world, digital storytelling does not merely echo tradition—it transforms into an ever-evolving canvas where human emotion and technological precision intertwine, painting tales of breathtaking complexity and depth. However, this transformative power comes with profound challenges. For example, the proliferation of deepfakes and AI-generated narratives strains the very fabric of truth and authenticity, demanding new forms of media literacy and verification. The rapid dissemination of misinformation and highly curated echo chambers, fueled by platform algorithms designed for engagement, can fracture shared realities and hinder critical discourse, posing a significant threat to collective understanding.

Furthermore, the ethical implications of AI-driven personalization raise questions about data privacy, manipulation, and the potential erosion of spontaneous discovery when narratives are constantly optimized to predict and confirm existing preferences. The increasing commodification of attention in digital spaces also shifts the incentives for narrative creation, potentially prioritizing fleeting viral appeal over depth or enduring meaning. As storytelling evolves, one must ask: How might these emerging forms reshape our sense of identity and connection, redefining how we engage with our personal and collective narratives, particularly as the lines between creator, algorithm, and audience continue to blur?

Chapter Nineteen
The Pattern-Seeking Society: Politics, Economics, and Social Change

From the dawn of civilization to the hyper-connected modern era, humankind has relentlessly sought to impose order on the inherent chaos of existence. This deep-seated drive to detect, interpret, and act upon recognizable patterns is not merely an isolated trait of individual psychology but a collective impulse that shapes entire societies. It runs through the veins of social movements, is embedded in the structures of political systems, and informs the rhythms of global economies and media narratives alike. This chapter investigates extensively how these pattern-seeking instincts shape public life—from micro-level interactions in protest rallies to the macro-level dynamics of political and economic cycles. It examines how collective behavior becomes a force for social change, how recurring economic trends reflect inherent human psychology and complex systemic dynamics, and how media and public perception draw upon familiar narratives that unite and polarize communities.

Almost instinctively, when events unfold—political upheavals, economic downturns, or cultural controversies—the collective mind gravitates toward familiar templates. Historical revolutions, such as the French Revolution and the Arab Spring, are recast as paradigms of cyclical renewal: oppressive regimes crumble, and in their place emerges a fervor for change. Society perceives these events as unfolding by an almost mythic ritual—a breaking point followed by chaos and, ideally, reformation. In moments of deep uncertainty—from economic recessions to political scandals—the collective instinct to detect familiar patterns offers comfort and a narrative framework for making sense of profound change. This urge, reassuring and galvanizing, fuels protest movements and rallies communities around common causes, setting the stage for transformative reforms. Sociologists studying social movements, such as Charles Tilly's work on "repertoires of contention," illustrate how activists adopt and adapt established forms of collective action that have proven effective historically, recognizing shared grievances and drawing upon a collective memory of past struggles. Contemporary examples like the global Fridays for Future climate strikes or the #MeToo movement demonstrate how digital platforms enable rapid pattern recognition and coordination, allowing for the widespread adoption of unified messaging and protest tactics, creating a powerful, identifiable wave of collective action. One might ask: When was a crisis first witnessed that catalyzed collective action by echoing time-honored cycles of decay and renewal?

These collective behaviors are powerfully reflected in the political arena. At their core, political ideologies are narratives—stories that explain identity, origin, and destiny. They routinely recycle decades, if not centuries, of shared history, framing events regarding hope, fear, and promise. Political parties craft platforms built on simplified, recurrent themes: the promise of a return to a "golden age," warnings of inevitable decline, or calls for radical reinvention. For instance, populist movements frequently capitalize on perceptions that established institutions have repeatedly failed, creating an "old-order versus reform" narrative that resonates deeply within the public psyche. Political scientists like Arthur Schlesinger Jr. famously documented cyclical patterns in American politics, from periods of public purpose to private interest. This pattern-seeking also manifests in the prevalence of "framing effects," a concept from communication theory, where political actors strategically present information in ways that align with pre-existing mental schemas and archetypal narratives, guiding public interpretation. In such cases, opinion polls, public rallies, and political debates become chapters in a recurring saga—a grand narrative in which leaders appear and vanish in cycles reminiscent of classic drama. As social media amplifies these patterns, political discussions increasingly echo through trending hashtags, viral videos, and online campaigns. Nevertheless, this same pattern-seeking force can inadvertently reinforce divisions when complex events are interpreted through oversimplified formulas that may overlook nuance or emerging evidence. This phenomenon is often exacerbated by cognitive biases like confirmation bias, where individuals selectively seek out information that confirms their existing political narratives, and the availability heuristic causes them to overemphasize easily recalled, often sensationalized, examples, contributing to deep political polarization.

Similarly, economic systems pulse with recognizable, recurring patterns. History shows that markets experience periods of exuberant expansion followed by dramatic contractions. Scholars—from Milton Friedman to contemporary behavioral economists—have posited that these cycles are influenced not only by mechanistic economic forces but also by collective moods, biases, and irrational overreactions inherent in human behavior. The boom-and-bust cycle, evidenced in phenomena from the Tulip Mania of the seventeenth century to the global financial crisis of 2007–2008, illustrates how optimism, overconfidence, and herd mentality drive investments and consumer behavior in predictable ways. Behavioral economics, building on insights from Kahneman and Tversky, specifically details how cognitive shortcuts like anchoring bias (over-reliance on initial information) and representativeness heuristic (judging by similarity to a stereotype) contribute to market bubbles and panics, leading investors to identify false patterns or misinterpret accurate signals. When a surge in optimism propels markets upward, the same forces tend to precipitate a drastic downturn as skepticism spreads and risk aversion takes hold. Such cycles vividly demonstrate the recurring nature of economic dynamics. It is worth reflecting on how periods of economic exuberance followed by downturns have impacted not only individual finances but also the broader social fabric during times of crisis.

The interplay of these recurring patterns also extends into media and public perception. In its multifaceted role as curator and interpreter of news, the media functions as a crucible in which complex events are distilled into symbolic narratives. Journalists, pundits, and digital platforms shape stories by emphasizing familiar themes—transforming isolated incidents into episodes emblematic of broader systemic trends, such as cycles of corruption followed by reform. For example, political scandals are frequently presented not solely in terms of their specific details but as evidence of an enduring narrative of institutional decay. Media theories such as Agenda-Setting, which posits that media determines what is important by what it covers, and Framing Theory, which focuses on how the media tells stories by emphasizing certain aspects, directly illuminate how narratives are constructed to align with public pattern recognition. The consistent portrayal of political figures as "heroes" or "villains" or economic downturns as "inevitable corrections" are potent examples of this. In an era of information overload, media framing guides public opinion, uniting communities around shared ideals or deepening divisions through simplified dichotomies. Sophisticated algorithms contribute by selectively amplifying content that aligns with established patterns, sometimes at the expense of nuance. One may wonder how familiar media frames have influenced interpretations of historical events or current crises.

At the confluence of collective behavior, economic cycles, and media narratives lies a profound synthesis—a vivid portrait of a pattern-seeking society. The innate drive to discern order in chaos provides a lens through which to understand the past, interpret the present, and project the future. However, this same impulse can also constrain thought to predetermined models, rendering the complexities of change into overly familiar formulas. Excessive reliance on recognized patterns risks reinforcing cycles of division, stagnation, and decline, as the collective memory becomes a self-fulfilling prophecy wherein the expectation of repeated outcomes shapes decisions that render those outcomes inevitable. A critical limitation of human pattern-seeking is its susceptibility to false positives or the imposition of patterns where none exist, often driven by a need for certainty. It can lead to a rigidity in thinking, where new or genuinely unprecedented events are forced into old frameworks, preventing adaptive responses and hindering true innovation. The challenge lies in distinguishing between genuine underlying rhythms and mere coincidence or avoiding the trap of recency bias, where short-term trends are mistakenly elevated to universal patterns.

Looking ahead, the challenge for a pattern-seeking society is to harness these instincts to drive positive change rather than to perpetuate outdated paradigms. Envision a future in which policymakers, economists, and media professionals collaborate with advanced data analytics, behavioral science, and artificial intelligence to perpetuate familiar narratives and innovate and transform. For example, imagine a governance model where real-time monitoring of public sentiment allows leaders to preempt crises before they escalate or economic policies that integrate behavioral insights to cushion the extremes of market cycles. Picture media ecosystems that combine diverse algorithmic inputs to present balanced, multifaceted narratives that foster informed and inclusive public discourse. Such advancements could transform pattern-seeking impulses from a predominantly reactive mechanism into a proactive tool for building equity, transparency, and sustainable progress.

It is a pattern-seeking society—a civilization defined by an enduring quest for order and meaning amid turbulence. Every protest against perceived injustice, every phase of economic expansion or contraction, and every media narrative that comes to prominence expresses the deep-seated drive to discern recurring themes from the chaos of modern life. However, within these recurring cycles lies the potential for renewal; through careful discernment, it is possible to break free from destructive patterns and create new paradigms that are more equitable and resilient. It necessitates recognizing patterns and actively questioning their applicability, seeking out disconfirming evidence, and embracing the "black swan" events that fundamentally challenge established norms. Identifying, adapting, and deliberately breaking from entrenched patterns becomes the hallmark of a truly resilient and evolving society, allowing for innovation that transcends deterministic cycles.

In contemplating the interplay of these forces, it becomes clear that recognizing recurring patterns is not an exercise in determinism but rather a means of empowering deliberate change. Observing how cycles in political revolutions, market behaviors, and media narratives have shaped collective destiny offers valuable insights for constructing more resilient institutions, more adaptive economic systems, and a public discourse that embraces complexity rather than reducing issues to simplistic dichotomies. The awareness of these recurring themes provides a foundation upon which systemic reforms can be built—a foundation that honors historical legacy while paving the way for innovation.

The insights gleaned from this exploration will nurture critical engagement with the many forces shaping modern society. Understanding the recurring cycles that define political, economic, and media landscapes makes it possible to contribute meaningfully to creating a future transcending divisive repetition. Recognizing patterns can catalyze progress—a tool to foster unity, encourage nuanced discourse, and build a more transparent and adaptable global community.

The pattern-seeking society is an ever-evolving organism in which the search for order amid unpredictability remains a driving force. The endless dance of cycles that define political, economic, and cultural landscapes offers continuous opportunities for reinvention. Every revolution, every market fluctuation, and every media narrative forms part of a vast, intricate tapestry of human progress. When recurring patterns are recognized, questioned, and transformed, they yield the potential to write new narratives—ones that are innovative, inclusive, and transformative.

May the reflections herein inspire a commitment to critically engaging with contemporary challenges. The ideas presented will empower all who study these themes to participate constructively in the ongoing process of societal evolution. Recognizing and understanding the repeating rhythms of collective behavior is not merely an academic exercise but a vital contribution to shaping a future defined by resilience and hope. This pattern-seeking society is a living testament to the enduring search for order amid uncertainty, a chronicle of cycles and revolutions, and a clarion call to transform recurring narratives into a dynamic future. In the unending interplay of tradition and innovation, every insight into pattern recognition forms a critical thread in the tapestry of shared destiny, ensuring that the legacy of the past continues to illuminate the path forward.

Chapter Twenty
Virtual and Augmented Reality: The New Frontier of Perception

From the earliest myths of immersive journeys in literature and art to today's most advanced digital simulations, humankind has ceaselessly sought to transcend physical boundaries. Whether through oral storytelling, theatrical illusions, or virtual landscapes, the impulse to construct alternate realms has been a defining characteristic of human creativity. In the past, grand epic traditions carried stories that immersed listeners so deeply that reality blurred with imagination. In the modern world, the same instinct drives the advancement of virtual and augmented reality—technologies that do more than entertain; they redefine perception. By engaging the brain's pattern-recognition faculties, these immersive experiences tap into the mechanisms that shape human cognition, memory, and identity.

The human mind has always been drawn to structured narratives. Whether encountering ancient sagas or modern interactive digital environments, there is an innate tendency to seek meaning in sensory experiences. Studies suggest that immersion—whether in a richly detailed novel, an intricately painted fresco, or a fully realized digital simulation—works not through the mere presentation of information but through the brain's ability to synthesize patterns, anticipate outcomes, and embed memory within structured realities. Virtual reality leverages this phenomenon by employing high-resolution visuals, stereoscopic 3D rendering, spatial audio, and haptic feedback. These elements work together to generate an environment the mind interprets as genuine despite knowing it is artificial. This cognitive phenomenon is often described in terms of "presence" or "telepresence" by VR researchers, where the user's perceptual system is convinced of being physically located within the virtual environment, even when the rational mind knows otherwise. It involves tricking the brain's proprioception and vestibular system through precise sensor synchronization and low latency. Users of deeply immersive systems often report alterations in their perception of time, a phenomenon traced to how digital environments override traditional sensory markers. Some virtual experiences create an intensified perception of time, where hours feel like minutes, while others disrupt time awareness entirely, plunging users into a state of extended presence. Augmented reality operates similarly, seamlessly integrating digital overlays into physical surroundings, creating an interface between the organic and the synthetic that reshapes how humans interpret space.

Immersive spaces extend beyond solitary experience. Multi-user virtual environments allow participants to enter shared digital worlds where gestures, spatial audio positioning, and intelligent avatars facilitate interactions rival real-world social engagement. Entire virtual classrooms, collaborative workspaces, and simulated artistic studios now enable individuals across vast distances to engage meaningfully without the limitations of physical presence. Platforms like Meta's Horizon Workrooms or the growing popularity of virtual concerts in games like Fortnite demonstrate how sophisticated network protocols and rendering engines create a convincing shared social presence. This connectivity draws upon deep-rooted human behaviors—social learning, mimicry, and environmental adaptation—that have historically shaped civilizations. In ancient societies, communal storytelling defined cultural continuity and collective identity; today, digital collaboration platforms have assumed that role, creating new forms of cultural expression and redefining the foundations of social exchange.

Underlying these immersive experiences is a discipline known as cognitive ergonomics, which ensures that digital environments harmonize with the brain's natural processing capabilities. The mind instinctively seeks structure in chaos, forming patterns in unpredictable data. Immersive designers capitalize on this by crafting intuitive digital interfaces, ensuring that navigation, visual hierarchies, and sensory feedback align seamlessly with human cognitive expectations. When immersive spaces align with these natural tendencies, they allow users to engage effortlessly, experiencing presence without disruption. Algorithms refine these processes further, analyzing biometric responses—eye movements, heart rate fluctuations, and micro-expressions—to adapt the content in real-time. This dynamic personalization improves comfort, reducing motion sickness while deepening engagement. However, ethical concerns arise when persuasive design strategies exploit cognitive biases, such as framing effects or the mere-exposure effect, subtly influencing decisions in ways users may not consciously recognize, moving beyond simple engagement to potential manipulation. This area, often explored within the field of "persuasive technology" or "dark patterns," highlights how the very effectiveness of immersive design can become an ethical minefield, impacting user autonomy. The psychological implications of immersive persuasion necessitate careful regulation as virtual interactions become more embedded in daily life.

The integration of virtual and augmented realities carries profound societal implications. Education systems have begun leveraging these technologies to create history simulations, interactive science laboratories, and adaptive language learning spaces that modify instruction according to an individual's cognitive engagement. For example, medical schools increasingly use VR platforms for surgical training, allowing students to practice complex procedures in a risk-free environment. At the same time, companies like Immersive VR Education's "Apollo 11 VR" offer highly engaging historical experiences. Healthcare has equally embraced the technology, using VR-assisted surgeries, neurological rehabilitation programs (e.g., for stroke recovery), and psychological therapy simulations (e.g., exposure therapy for phobias) to address medical challenges in innovative ways. These advances hold the promise of bridging inequities in access, particularly in underserved regions where traditional infrastructure fails to provide adequate educational and medical resources. However, concerns about digital dependency, prolonged exposure to artificial environments, and memory alteration demand careful study. The potential for "virtual reality sickness" (cybersickness), the psychological impact of spending extensive time in virtual worlds (e.g., effects on social skills in the physical world), and the blurring of real vs. virtual memories (e.g., false memory creation or source confusion) are active research areas in human-computer interaction and psychology, raising questions about long-term neurological and behavioral effects. As more aspects of life transition into immersive formats, society must grapple with the shifting boundaries between what is experienced digitally and what is considered authentic.

Economically, immersive technology is revolutionizing traditional markets, introducing new models of commerce that challenge existing paradigms. Digital assets such as virtual real estate, interactive experiences, and even algorithm-generated fashion designs hold real monetary value, reshaping how consumers engage with goods and services. The emergence of immersive retail spaces enables customers to browse fully realized digital storefronts, interact with AI-driven personal shoppers, and test products virtually before purchasing physical versions. The growth of the metaverse and NFTs (Non-Fungible Tokens) are prime examples, where unique digital items are bought and sold, creating entirely new economic ecosystems with distinct value propositions. For instance, brands like Gucci and Nike have launched virtual fashion lines and digital collectibles within platforms like Roblox and Decentraland, challenging conventional supply chains and consumer behavior. In the entertainment and gaming industries, digital economies thrive on customizable avatars, virtual concerts, and algorithm-driven events, redefining the meaning of ownership and consumer experience. As these markets expand, legal and ethical frameworks must evolve to accommodate the complexities of digital trade, ensuring accountability in virtual transactions and safeguarding consumer rights in environments where traditional laws struggle to apply. The lack of established legal precedents for digital property rights, intellectual property ownership of AI-generated content, and consumer protection in decentralized virtual economies represents significant regulatory challenges.

Political and cultural institutions likewise adapt to immersive technology, employing digital simulations to visualize policy decisions, forecast societal trends, and enhance public engagement. Virtual town halls allow citizens to participate in political discourse, examining interactive models of proposed legislation or experiencing firsthand the consequences of urban planning projects through VR simulations. For example, urban planners use AR overlays to visualize proposed building developments on existing cityscapes, allowing for more informed public input. At the same time, VR experiences can simulate the impacts of climate change or natural disasters to foster empathy and drive policy support. Nevertheless, with increased immersion comes the risk of manipulation. Carefully curated digital environments can influence public perception, shaping opinions through hyper-realistic yet selectively framed experiences. The phenomenon of virtual propaganda—immersive narratives designed to engineer consent—presents unprecedented ethical dilemmas, requiring societies to develop safeguards against misinformation in immersive media. The potential for deepfake technology, combined with immersive environments, to create compelling but entirely fabricated events or political speeches raises serious concerns about the integrity of information and the susceptibility of public opinion to engineered realities. It necessitates advanced digital forensics, robust media literacy programs, and clear ethical guidelines for designing and deploying immersive communication platforms. As digital landscapes become arenas for ideological battles, the need for media literacy and transparent digital governance grows increasingly urgent.

The trajectory of immersive technology suggests that it will not merely supplement existing realities but will evolve into an integral dimension of human existence. As VR and AR integrate into everyday routines, their influence on identity formation, cognitive adaptability, and interpersonal relationships will deepen. Ethical debates surrounding agency, privacy, and the psychological effects of prolonged engagement will shape policies and cultural attitudes toward immersive technology. The dialogue between engineered environments and human intuition presents an opportunity to ensure that these innovations foster collective progress rather than erode the foundations of independent thought.

Tracing its lineage from ancient myths to today's computational landscapes, immersive technology represents a profound shift in how humans experience reality. By harnessing the brain's pattern-recognition faculties, VR and AR challenge traditional sensory structures, creating experiences that transcend existing cognitive models. What existed solely within storytelling traditions now unfolds through digital immersion, forming environments where history, science, art, and philosophy converge. These technologies are designed to entertain and transform, offering new realms of exploration that bridge narrative pasts with computational futures. With every innovation, ethical discourse, and immersive experiment, humanity moves further into an era where simulation, perception, and memory blend into an intricate, expanding experience network. What once seemed distant speculation of technological advancement is now the foundation of an evolving reality woven from the essence of human storytelling and the precision of digital craftsmanship.

Chapter Twenty-One
The Neurochemical Underpinnings of Pattern Recognition

The human brain is an extraordinary organ that transforms sensory data streams into coherent perceptions, vivid memories, and creative insights. Central to this ability is pattern recognition—the process by which organized sequences and configurations are detected and interpreted. This chapter investigates the neurochemical foundations of this process by examining how neurotransmitters influence satisfaction and motivation during pattern recognition, how altered states of consciousness modify these processes, and how neuroplasticity enables the brain to adapt by reinforcing or restructuring established perceptual patterns.

Neurotransmitters serve as critical mediators in pattern recognition. Dopamine, often described as the "reward" molecule, reinforces neural activity when familiar configurations are encountered. The mesolimbic pathway—encompassing regions such as the ventral tegmental area and the nucleus accumbens—responds to patterns with bursts of dopamine, which creates a sense of pleasure and strengthens the neural circuits that process these stimuli. In parallel, serotonin contributes to mood regulation and cognitive flexibility by modulating the intensity and stability of dopaminergic responses. The balance between dopamine's energizing drive and serotonin's regulatory influence is essential; it reinforces frequently encountered patterns and the openness necessary to integrate novel information into enduring cognitive frameworks. Beyond these, other crucial neuromodulators like norepinephrine, which enhances attention and novelty detection, and acetylcholine, vital for memory encoding and synaptic plasticity, also play significant roles, contributing to the brain's ability to focus on and consolidate new patterns.

Numerous imaging studies support these roles. For instance, tasks requiring sequence identification consistently increase dopaminergic activity, which correlates with improved reaction times and accuracy. In conditions marked by dopamine deficits, such as Parkinson's disease, difficulties arise in processing complex stimuli. Meanwhile, fluctuating serotonergic activity influences cognitive flexibility, enabling the brain to maintain or adjust existing patterns in response to new data. Beyond subcortical regions like the mesolimbic pathway, complex pattern recognition relies heavily on the orchestrated activity of cortical areas. The prefrontal cortex, for example, is critical for detecting abstract patterns and rule-based learning, while the temporal lobe excels in visual pattern recognition and object identification. The parietal cortex contributes by managing spatial patterns and directing attentional shifts between different pattern features. Distributed processing highlights that pattern recognition is not localized but emerges from the dynamic interplay across multiple brain networks.

Altered states of consciousness provide insight into the brain's flexibility in recognizing and reinterpreting patterns. Deep meditation reduces the background noise of consciousness, allowing less dominant neural pathways to emerge and reveal subtle internal configurations. Neuroimaging research has shown that meditation suppresses the default mode network (DMN) activity, enhancing connections between regions responsible for attention and pattern detection. During rapid eye movement (REM) sleep, the brain processes sensory and emotional information non-linearly, producing dreams in which disparate elements may merge into novel associations. These changes in neural connectivity not only facilitate memory consolidation but may also contribute to creative problem-solving. Psychedelic substances, which interact primarily with serotonin receptors such as the 5-HT2A receptor, profoundly reorganize neural activity. The resulting increase in neural entropy dissolves conventional sensory boundaries. It permits more fluid associations between concepts, often yielding transformative insights and novel creative expressions by fostering enhanced communication across otherwise segregated brain networks.

Neuroplasticity—the brain's remarkable ability to reorganize itself by forming new neural connections—is essential to adapting cognitive frameworks, reinforcing learning, and generating creative insights. When particular patterns are repeatedly encountered, synaptic connections strengthen through long-term potentiation (LTP), making recognition more efficient. This adaptive process underlies routine behavior and habit formation. Simultaneously, exposure to novel stimuli can prompt the formation of alternate neural pathways, effectively challenging and reshaping preexisting patterns. The perpetual reorganization of synaptic networks ensures that learning is dynamic and adaptable, paving the way for creative breakthroughs when conventional frameworks no longer suffice. This adaptive process is fundamentally rooted in Hebbian learning principles—"neurons that fire together wire together"—and is increasingly understood through computational models like predictive coding, where the brain continuously generates and refines internal models of the world by predicting incoming sensory information and updating its patterns when predictions are violated.

The ability to acquire knowledge, refine skills, and adapt to changing circumstances hinges on neuroplasticity. Embracing new challenges and varied learning experiences ensures cognitive agility and prevents stagnation. Picking up a new language, playing a musical instrument, or engaging in creative writing prompts the brain to develop new connections, enhancing problem-solving ability and mental flexibility. Learning a new language introduces intricate grammatical structures, phonetic associations, and cultural contexts, requiring the brain to forge new synaptic pathways while improving memory and comprehension. Likewise, playing an instrument involves the simultaneous activation of motor coordination, auditory processing, and emotional interpretation, reinforcing neural networks that enhance multitasking and creativity. Through narrative construction and linguistic manipulation, creative writing encourages the brain to weave abstract concepts into structured expression, strengthening cognitive fluidity and imaginative problem-solving.

Exposure to multiple disciplines fosters cognitive resilience and adaptability by encouraging the brain to synthesize diverse forms of knowledge. Integrating insights across varied fields—such as merging scientific principles with artistic creativity or blending historical perspectives with technological advancements—creates more adaptable neural networks, allowing for innovative thinking and problem-solving. Cross-disciplinary engagement sharpens mental agility, helping individuals recognize patterns across domains and apply flexible reasoning to complex situations. Reading philosophy alongside mathematics or studying literature with physics cultivates intellectual dexterity, reinforcing the brain's ability to navigate and integrate broad intellectual landscapes.

Mental workouts, including puzzle-solving, logic-based challenges, and memory exercises, provide structured opportunities to refine cognitive precision. Games such as chess and Sudoku demand strategic planning and foresight, training the brain to anticipate multiple outcomes while honing analytical reasoning. Memory-based exercises strengthen recall mechanisms by engaging repetition and retrieval strategies that reinforce synaptic connections. By consistently engaging in cognitive challenges, individuals improve focus, enhance reaction times, and build resilience against cognitive decline. The discipline of pattern recognition is deeply intertwined with these mental exercises, ensuring that the brain remains agile and adaptive throughout life.

These neurochemical and structural processes are fundamental to everyday cognition and explain extraordinary moments of insight. The pleasure derived from perceiving balance in a work of art or the satisfaction accompanying the resolution of a complex problem is rooted in the interplay between dopamine-induced reward signals and the reinforcement of neural circuits specialized for pattern detection. Such sudden insight—often described as "eureka" experiences—arises when the brain successfully integrates disparate data into a coherent whole and encodes this new association for future use.

The implications of these processes extend to multiple domains. Alterations in neurotransmitter balance can significantly affect mental health; imbalances in dopamine and serotonin are associated with disorders such as depression, anxiety, and obsessive-compulsive behaviors, all of which can disrupt the capacity to process and interpret patterns. Therapeutic interventions that restore neurochemical balance and activities designed to stimulate neuroplasticity hold promise for enhancing cognitive flexibility and alleviating symptoms of such disorders. In education, strategies that leverage neuroplasticity—such as spaced repetition and multimodal learning—can enhance the acquisition and retention of new information by aligning with the brain's natural methods for reinforcing patterns. Furthermore, understanding these mechanisms allows us to explore the vast spectrum of individual differences in pattern recognition, from the enhanced detail processing sometimes observed in autism spectrum disorder to the unique cognitive profiles seen in savant syndrome, illustrating the brain's diverse adaptive capacities.

Neuroimaging and computational modeling advances continue to shed light on the intricate neural networks underpinning pattern recognition. These methods reveal that the interplay between neurotransmitter release, altered states of consciousness, and synaptic reorganization is highly dynamic, evolving continuously in response to accumulating experience. Ongoing research lays the groundwork for personalized cognitive enhancement techniques, where interventions are tailored to an individual's unique neural activation patterns, potentially boosting creative output and problem-solving capabilities. It includes investigating how these processes develop from infancy, as the brain gradually builds its repertoire of patterns through early sensory and motor experiences, shaping the fundamental architecture for later complex cognition.

In summary, the neurochemical underpinnings of pattern recognition constitute a complex and interdependent system essential to human cognition. The well-coordinated release of dopamine and serotonin provides both the drive to detect familiar configurations and the flexibility to update them in light of new experiences. Altered states of consciousness—whether brought about by meditation, sleep, or psychedelics—demonstrate that the brain's approach to processing patterns is not fixed but highly adaptable. Repeated exposure to stimuli through neuroplasticity refines these processes, ensuring that learning remains efficient and innovative. These adaptive mechanisms underpin routine cognitive functions, laying the foundation for creative breakthroughs and lifelong learning.

Understanding these mechanisms offers profound insights into the nature of human thought and creativity. By elucidating how the brain detects, reinforces, and transforms patterns, it becomes possible to envision new approaches to mental health, education, and artistic expression. As research continues to illuminate the dynamic interplay between neurochemistry and neuroplasticity, future applications may include personalized cognitive training, novel therapeutic strategies for mental disorders, and innovative educational programs designed to harness the brain's full creative potential. Integrating these advances promises to improve our understanding of human cognition and foster environments that support continued cognitive growth and creativity. This comprehensive exploration of the neurochemical basis of pattern recognition underscores its central role in shaping perception, memory, and creativity. The intricate balance of neurotransmitters and the brain's remarkable capacity for adaptation reveal a robust and flexible system capable of transforming chaotic inputs into meaningful experiences. As the study of these processes advances, the potential to enhance cognitive function and spark innovative ideas will undoubtedly expand, offering exciting avenues for future discovery and application. The dynamic interplay of chemical signals and neural adaptation remains fundamental to the development of human intelligence, serving as the foundation upon which the endless capacity for learning and creative thought is built.

Chapter Twenty-Two

Patterns and the Human Experience: Meaning, Mystery, and the Quest for Purpose

An ancient and irresistible force compels the human spirit to seek order amid chaos in a world that often appears as a swirling maelstrom of unpredictability and relentless change. At the very moment when life seems to unravel into countless random fragments, a deep and almost primordial urge arises to uncover hidden symmetries and elusive patterns—a call that has echoed throughout millennia and forged the foundations of myth, art, and philosophy. When arbitrary events appear, this instinct to detect order turns the disjointed and formless into a coherent narrative that offers hope and a sense of purpose. Every heartbeat, every starlit night, and every whispered legend testifies to this enduring attraction, suggesting that even amid apparent randomness, there lies an underlying tapestry of meaning waiting to be deciphered.

Since the earliest days of human expression, civilizations have grappled with the inscrutable forces of existence by fashioning elaborate narratives that meld the tangible with the transcendent. Prehistoric cave paintings, etched symbols on ancient stones, and the storied oral traditions of early societies all reveal a consistent pattern: an instinctive inclination to interpret natural cycles—birth and death, light and darkness, decay and renewal—as expressions of a deeper cosmic order. Early mythologies did not view chance as the sole ruler of fate; instead, they celebrated the idea that the manifold events of life were integral parts of a grand design. Philosophers from the Stoics to the existentialists posited that beneath the surface of chaos, a hidden blueprint might govern the universe—a blueprint that provides solace in the face of uncertainty and connects personal suffering with the possibility of transformation. This quest for existential patterns is often explored through theories like Victor Frankl's logotherapy, which posits a fundamental "will to meaning" as a primary human motivator, or cognitive dissonance theory, which explains how individuals strive for coherence between their beliefs and experiences, far from being a mere intellectual exercise, forms the essence of the human condition, transforming disorientation into a quest for clarity.

Central to this search is the timeless power of symbols and myth. Across diverse cultures, recurring images and archetypes have emerged as condensed, potent embodiments of shared human experience. The archetypal hero, the eternal serpent, the labyrinth, and the cyclical motif of the seasons transcend geographical and temporal boundaries, resonating with fundamental aspects of the collective psyche. Carl Jung's concept of the collective unconscious speaks explicitly to these universal archetypes, suggesting an innate human predisposition to understand the world through these symbolic patterns. These symbols function on multiple levels—they provide a common language through which profound truths are communicated, serve as repositories of collective memory, and offer frameworks within which societies articulate values and ideals. The hero's journey, for example, recurs in myriad forms as a metaphor for personal transformation. This narrative of struggle, sacrifice, and, ultimately, renewal unites disparate cultures and grants individuals a means to recast personal adversities as pivotal episodes in a larger saga of redemption. However, while such symbols often provide comfort and continuity, there is also a risk: if revered uncritically, these timeless forms can constrain innovative thought and bind perceptions to outdated paradigms. This uncritical reverence can lead to cultural stagnation or dogmatism, as societies resist new realities by rigidly adhering to established, often simplistic, frameworks. History shows how the co-optation of powerful national myths, for instance, can justify conflict or oppression when their inherent patterns are presented as unquestionable truths, overlooking nuance or emerging evidence that challenges the sacred narrative. The tension between the stabilizing influence of familiar myths and the inherent need to question and evolve these symbols lies at the heart of ongoing cultural renewal.

The quest for meaning has assumed new dimensions as ancient symbols merge with contemporary aspirations. The rapid advance of technology and the relentless pace of modern life have renewed interest in practices that nurture inner reflection and self-awareness. Contemporary spirituality—embodied in practices such as mindfulness, meditation, and yoga—draws upon ancient ritual's power while engaging with modern science's insights. In an age of data and constant stimulation, these practices offer a deliberate pause, inviting the mind to sift through clashing signals and discern the underlying patterns that govern thought, emotion, and perception. Digital platforms have further democratized this inner search, with apps like Calm and Headspace and virtual communities providing accessible pathways to practices once reserved for monastic or esoteric traditions. Beyond accessibility, digital technologies offer new lenses for meaning-making: Visualizing vast datasets can reveal previously invisible patterns in complex systems, fostering new understandings of societal trends or ecological dynamics. Furthermore, algorithmic pattern recognition in areas like personalized content feeds, while posing challenges of echo chambers, also introduces individuals to new forms of "order" in information consumption, influencing their daily construction of meaning. The modern spiritual quest is not a rejection of modernity; rather, it is an evolved response to the existential challenges of a hyper-connected world, replete with uncertainties yet rich with possibilities.

This fusion of ancient wisdom and modern insight is apparent not only on an individual level but also in our time's collective cultural and artistic expressions. Contemporary art, literature, and music frequently echo the archetypal themes of sacrifice, transformation, and eternal recurrence. Across canvases, pages, and soundscapes, creative works distill the complexity of existence into expressions that speak to both the rational mind and the depths of emotion. Such works do more than merely illustrate the search for meaning—they embody it, offering audiences visceral experiences that both comfort and provoke. The interplay between tradition and innovation is palpable in these expressions: age-old myths are reinterpreted through modern aesthetics, and familiar symbols are repurposed to address the present dilemmas. The emergence of new, culturally significant symbols can be observed in contemporary social movements, where viral hashtags like #BlackLivesMatter or specific visual cues like the raised fist rapidly become powerful, unifying symbols of shared identity and purpose, demonstrating how collective experience in the digital age can quickly forge new archetypal representations. The result is an ever-evolving dialogue between past and present, where the enduring symbols of earlier eras are imbued with fresh relevance and transformative potential.

At the societal level, the search for meaning in recurring patterns exerts a powerful influence over collective consciousness and cultural norms. In times of crisis or rapid change, societies often turn to established symbols and archetypes as anchors to provide stability and direction. The narratives of struggle and renewal that have sustained communities for generations become instrumental in rallying people together, whether in the form of national myths, religious rituals, or grassroots movements advocating for social justice or environmental stewardship. These shared narratives offer a common framework that explains the vicissitudes of life and inspires collective action. Nevertheless, the influence of these enduring patterns is dual-edged. At the same time, they can foster unity, but they may also hinder progress if they prevent the adoption of innovative perspectives that challenge outdated traditions. The sociological concept of "cultural inertia" describes how deeply embedded patterns of thought and behavior resist change, even when faced with new evidence. It can lead to resistance to necessary social reforms, particularly when alternative narratives threaten deeply ingrained mythologies or power structures. Critiques from postmodern thought, for instance, challenge the notion of a single, universal grand narrative, arguing that such attempts to impose overarching order can suppress diverse perspectives and lead to epistemological rigidity.

On an individual level, the intrinsic need to uncover order in chaos is both a path to personal growth and an ongoing source of creative inspiration. The journey toward self-understanding is marked by moments of exquisite clarity and profound uncertainty. Personal transformation often arises from the reexamination of deeply held beliefs and the confrontation of long-standing inner conflicts. Whether encountered in solitary meditation, therapeutic dialogue, or immersive artistic creation, these moments of insight—those "eureka" experiences—are fueled by the same fundamental impulse to see beyond the surface of randomness. The resulting inner alchemy transforms vulnerability and chaos into wisdom and new possibilities, enabling individuals to draft new, adaptive, and deeply authentic narratives for their lives.

With its unique blend of challenges and opportunities, the modern era has intensified the timeless quest for meaning. Globalization, environmental crises, and rapid technological advancements have heightened the need for coherent, meaningful narratives. In response, modern intellectuals, artists, and spiritual seekers are continuously reimagining tradition to honor the past while addressing present demands. The emerging cultural mosaic is where ancient archetypes coexist with modern symbols of innovation and progress, each contributing to a nuanced collective vision of purposeful living. This synthesis is not static; it evolves as society grapples with new realities, ensuring the search for meaning remains active, dynamic, reflective, and forward-looking.

The transformative power of this enduring quest becomes evident in the myriad ways that art and literature have captured the essence of the human condition. Masterpieces that span from the epic poems of antiquity to contemporary novels and films serve as mirrors reflecting the multifaceted journey of humanity. These creative endeavors invite introspection and foster a sense of shared destiny as recurring themes of heroism, sacrifice, and renewal resonate across diverse audiences. The narrative power of art to evoke empathy and inspire change underscores the pivotal role of mythic symbolism in shaping personal identity and collective values. Here, every gesture—every brushstroke, every carefully chosen word—contributes to an expansive dialogue that spans generations and cultures, reaffirming that the pursuit of meaning is not confined to isolated moments of insight but is woven into the fabric of human experience.

The interplay between existential inquiry, cultural symbolism, and the modern quest for spiritual awakening reveals that the search for meaning has always been a journey of individual transformation and collective evolution. In the quiet moments of introspection, when old narratives are questioned, and new possibilities emerge, seeking order in chaos becomes a mode of self-reinvention. This restless, ongoing process is emblematic of the creative spirit that thrives on the tension between certainty and doubt, tradition and innovation. It is a dialogue without end that challenges the mind, enlivens the heart, and continually redefines what it means to live a life of purpose.

In summary, the quest for meaning amid life's randomness is as vital now as it was in the days of our earliest ancestors. The intricate dance between ancient symbolism, philosophical reflection, and modern spiritual practice forms a rich tapestry that illustrates the perpetual human desire to understand, transform, and transcend. As the complexities of the contemporary world deepen the need for coherent narratives, the timeless journey to uncover hidden patterns endures—a journey that provides hope, inspires creativity, and defines the essence of the human spirit. In embracing this quest, individuals and communities reaffirm their capacity for renewal and highlight the endless potential for growth, connection, and transformation.

The exploration presented in this chapter is a testament to the enduring power of the human search for meaning—a beacon of light in a chaotic world, illuminating the beauty and mystery underlying every facet of existence. Every symbol reimagined, every myth retold, and every reflective moment bolsters the belief that even amid uncertainty, there lies an order that is both profound and life-affirming. The quest for purpose, in all its wonder and complexity, weaves together the ancient and the modern, the empirical and the mystical, into an unbroken narrative that continues to guide humanity toward greater understanding and Enlightenment. In the final analysis, pursuing patterns in "the human experience" is not merely an intellectual exercise but a vibrant, living process. This journey transcends the boundaries of time and culture to reveal the limitless potential inherent in every individual and every society. It is a journey that calls on the collective memory of the past and the innovative spirit of the future, forging a timeless connection between what has been and what might yet be. With all its paradoxes and possibilities, this inexhaustible quest remains an enduring testament to the human soul's creative, resilient, and transformative power.

Chapter Twenty-Three
Patterns in History — Repeating Cycles and the Illusion of Progress

The human impulse to find order and coherence in the seemingly chaotic flow of history has inspired profound reflection on whether the patterns observed—such as the rise and fall of civilizations or the oscillations of economies—reflect intrinsic laws governing societies or mere artifacts of human perception. Across cultures and eras, many traditions have embraced a cyclical view of time, seeing history not as a linear progression but as a series of recurring epochs. These views manifest in the Hindu concept of yugas, marked by stages of creation and destruction, and the Chinese cosmological cycles reflecting eternal renewal. Ancient thinkers like Polybius described political systems cycling through monarchy, oligarchy, and democracy, and Ibn Khalun analyzed the rise and decay of dynasties through internal and external pressures, illustrating that collapse and renewal are longstanding themes in human history. Modern scholars such as Oswald Spengler and Arnold Toynbee expanded this to a broad cyclical theory of civilizations moving through phases of birth, peak, decline, and rebirth, suggesting a rhythmic nature to social development.

At the same time, interpretation of history as a sequence of repetitive cycles has faced considerable criticism. The risk of confirmation bias means people may perceive patterns that confirm their expectations while ignoring anomalies. For instance, while the Roman Empire's decline is often cited as an archetype of inevitable decay, detailed study reveals a complex interplay of unique factors such as administrative challenges and external invasions. Economic episodes like the tulip mania or the Great Depression share traits of boom and bust, yet they differ fundamentally in underlying causes and contexts, challenging simplistic cyclical interpretations.

This tension between cyclic and linear narratives lies at the heart of historiography and influences how societies understand their trajectory. Historicism posits that broad, impersonal forces induce cyclical patterns—seen in economic models like Kondratiev's long waves of innovation and Juglar's business cycles—that shape political and economic developments. Conversely, accounts emphasizing linear progress highlight human creativity, innovation, and reform as driving forces that propel civilization forward beyond repetitive patterns. Critics such as Karl Popper have warned that deterministic views of history risk undermining human agency, encouraging fatalism and discouraging transformative action.

Examples vividly illustrate both perspectives. The Roman Empire's transformation and decline reflect both cyclic aspects of political entropy and unique historical contingencies; similarly, parallels can be drawn between various empires like Byzantium and the British Empire, but each presents distinctive transitions. Economic crises through history reveal recurring dynamics of speculation and collapse, though the specifics vary widely. Such multifaceted examples underscore that while recognizing patterns is valuable, it is essential to integrate the diversity and unpredictability of historical phenomena.

Applied thoughtfully, awareness of historical cycles carries practical benefits. Policymakers leverage cyclical insights to anticipate economic downturns and social unrest, developing regulatory frameworks like the Dodd-Frank Act to mitigate financial crises. Political leaders monitor trends in institutional trust and governance to design reforms enhancing resilience. Urban planners account for demographic and resource-use cycles to build cities capable of withstanding environmental challenges. At the same time, recognizing the limits of cyclical thinking guards against complacency and overgeneralization.

In sum, the study of recurring historical cycles reveals a rich interplay between enduring rhythms and contingent novelty. While cycles can inform wisdom and preparedness, history remains characterized by innovation, contingency, and human agency that may disrupt or transcend patterns. Understanding this balance enables societies to navigate complexity with flexibility—embracing the lessons of the past while remaining open to transformative change. Rather than viewing history as a fixed script of repetition, the awareness of patterns can empower humanity to choose paths of renewal and progress, crafting futures that honor enduring rhythms without succumbing to inevitability.

This nuanced exploration aligns with a broader cognitive tendency in humans: an innate drive to detect patterns in randomness, which both aids survival and shapes meaning-making but requires critical reflection to avoid misinterpretation. Thus, integrating historical pattern recognition with self-reflective awareness—recognizing our mental biases and narrative impulses—can foster more mindful engagement with the past and future.

Chapter Twenty-Four
Metacognition — Repeating Cycles, the Illusion of Progress, and the Reflexive Search for Patterns

In a world that can seem as chaotic and unpredictable as a storm-tossed sea, an almost magnetic pull draws the human spirit toward order—an innate drive to discern recurring patterns in events that, at first glance, appear random. When entire civilizations seem to rise and fall with disconcerting regularity or economic fortunes surge and collapse in predetermined rhythms, the human mind is compelled to seek the hidden structure beneath apparent chaos. This chapter embarks on an exhaustive exploration of historical cycles and the illusion of progress, investigating whether such cycles are an inherent feature of human society or retrospective constructs while simultaneously delving into metacognition—the reflexive ability to perceive patterns in our thought processes. This narrative forms a comprehensive tapestry that illuminates collective progress and personal growth by interweaving cyclical theories, the debate between historicism and linear innovation, and the practical lessons drawn from history and introspection.

Scholars have pursued the mysterious language of history from the earliest records of human expression. Ancient theories—such as the Hindu concept of the yugas and the cyclic cosmologies intrinsic to Chinese thought—envision time not as a linear progression from genesis to an ultimate end but as a series of grand, recurring epochs. Within these frameworks, history unfolds in cycles of creation, flourishing, decay, and renewal, much like the predictable change of the seasons. Thinkers like Polybius noted that political systems tend to oscillate between forms of governance—monarchy, oligarchy, and democracy—while Ibn Khaldun's seminal analysis of dynastic longevity underscored how internal cohesion, when eroded by power struggles and external pressures, typically gives way to collapse—only for a new order to arise eventually. Advocates of cyclical theories, including later proponents like Oswald Spengler and Arnold J. Toynbee, hold that events—from the fall of empires to the recurrent ebb and flow of economic activity—follow an inherent, almost inexorable order, offering a framework for extracting wisdom from the past.

Building upon these theoretical foundations, vivid historical examples further illuminate how these cycles manifest in reality. Consider the Roman Empire: its early expansion, marked by republican virtues and military prowess, later succumbed to a confluence of factors, including administrative overextension, fiscal mismanagement, political infighting, and relentless external pressures. Detailed examinations show how such forces converged to precipitate the decline of Rome—a pattern that, compared with the fates of Byzantium and other empires, suggests a recurring narrative of rise, peak, and decay. Similarly, economic phenomena provide robust illustrations of cyclical behavior. The speculative fervor during the Tulip Mania of 17th-century Holland, in which tulip bulb prices soared to unprecedented heights only to collapse dramatically, finds echoes in modern financial crises, such as the 2008 market downturn, where similar forces of exuberance, speculation, and inevitable correction played out on a grand scale. These historical economic recurrences are often analyzed through specific theoretical lenses, such as Kondratiev waves for long-term technological and economic cycles or Juglar cycles focusing on business investment fluctuations. These richly detailed accounts serve not only to anchor abstract theories in tangible experience but also to emphasize that while common motifs persist, each instance is colored by unique and complex underlying factors.

However, interpreting history as a series of cycles invites a debate between two contrasting narratives. On the one hand, historicism champions the notion that specific cycles are an inescapable aspect of human society, driven by enduring forces such as the consolidation of power, resource depletion, and institutional decay. Proponents argue that repeated political upheaval and economic volatility reflect fundamental laws of human behavior that naturally give rise to cyclic recurrence. On the other hand, advocates of linear progress assert that, despite the appearance of recurring motifs, human history is characterized by cumulative advancement. Each generation builds upon the legacy of its predecessors, harnessing knowledge and innovation to disrupt old patterns and forge unprecedented paths. The rapid strides in technology, medicine, and democratic governance over recent centuries testify to a transformative process that defies simplistic cyclical classification. This dialectic between the reassuring predictability of cyclical patterns and the promise of forward-moving progress is not only a scholarly debate—it informs contemporary political ideologies, economic policies, and societal strategies. Indeed, for many critical theorists, "progress" can be seen as an illusion. This comforting meta-narrative often obscures persistent inequalities, ecological degradation, or the cyclical re-emergence of fundamental human flaws like tribalism and greed, regardless of technological leaps. This perspective, often found in postmodern thought, challenges the notion that history's forward march inherently solves its most profound contradictions.

Recognizing historical cycles has significant practical implications for modern decision-making. Policymakers and economists, for example, study past economic boom-bust cycles to formulate preemptive measures that can mitigate the severity of downturns. Regulatory frameworks often emerge from lessons learned during episodes of financial instability, such as the Dodd-Frank Act following the 2008 financial crisis, guiding the design of interventions that stabilize markets and prevent crisis escalation. In the political arena, awareness of historical patterns in institutional decline and renewal informs efforts to safeguard governance structures against corruption, overreach, and internal discord. Urban planners and social policymakers also draw on cyclical theory to anticipate demographic shifts and resource allocation challenges, designing robust and adaptable systems. For instance, applying lessons from historical droughts and water management patterns can inform modern urban planning for climate resilience, while understanding the cyclical nature of public sentiment towards social reforms can guide strategic communication. The advent of big data and AI now allows for unprecedented computational analysis of historical patterns, offering new tools for foresight and even for creating predictive models in areas like financial markets or social unrest, although with inherent risks of algorithmic bias. Thus, by carefully analyzing past patterns, modern society can transform historical insights into actionable strategies for building resilient and innovative communities.

As the analysis of external historical trends comes to a close, the narrative invites an inward turn through the lens of metacognition. Metacognition—the capacity to reflect on one's thought processes—enables individuals to identify recurring patterns in their behavior and decision-making. By self-reflection, one can uncover habitual biases and cognitive shortcuts that influence interpreting external events. For instance, a propensity toward confirmation bias might lead one to selectively acknowledge evidence supporting inescapable cycles while discounting anomalies that defy such patterns. Recognizing these internal tendencies fosters greater self-awareness and sharpens one's ability to critically assess personal and collective narratives. Consider a business leader, deeply familiar with the historical patterns of market bubbles, who uses metacognition to identify their optimism bias during a period of irrational exuberance, prompting them to exercise caution and avoid joining the "herd mentality." Alternatively, recognizing their susceptibility to the narrative fallacy, a citizen might actively seek diverse news sources to avoid simplifying complex political crises into familiar "good vs. evil" cycles.

Mindfulness and cognitive therapy provide practical tools to enhance metacognitive awareness. Mindfulness meditation cultivates a nonjudgmental observation of present-moment experiences, allowing individuals to perceive subtle patterns in their thoughts and emotions. Cognitive therapy, with its systematic approach to identifying and restructuring maladaptive thought patterns, further empowers individuals to overcome ingrained biases. These practices underscore that the reflexive search for patterns within ourselves is as crucial as recognizing historical trends outside. The interplay here is profound: When scaled across a population, individual metacognition can directly influence the breaking of collective historical patterns by fostering collective critical thinking and a willingness to defy historical precedents. By integrating external wisdom with internal insight, individuals are better equipped to make decisions informed by past lessons while remaining open to transformative innovation.

Synthesizing the insights gleaned from historical cycles and metacognitive inquiry results in a balanced framework that acknowledges the value of recurring patterns while remaining alert to the forces of change and novelty. While history may present familiar motifs that serve as warnings and guides, the dynamic power of human creativity ensures that no event is entirely deterministic. When combined with deliberate self-reflection, recognizing cyclic recurrence allows societies and individuals to learn from previous errors, build upon past successes, and chart a course toward a future defined by adaptive progress.

In conclusion, the investigation of repeating cycles in history, when examined alongside the reflexive search for patterns in our thinking, reveals a multifaceted narrative of continuity and transformation. Historical episodes—from the decline of empires to the fluctuations of financial markets—offer a mirror reflecting humanity's enduring challenges and a map guiding future endeavors. Simultaneously, the disciplined practice of metacognition unveils personal insights that empower better decision-making and foster continuous self-improvement. Together, these twin avenues of inquiry remind us that while patterns may repeat, progress is not predetermined. The ultimate power lies in our collective and individual capacity to observe, question, and consciously interrupt these cycles—transforming inevitable recurrence into deliberate evolution. By embracing the lessons of the past and engaging in mindful self-reflection, modern society can transcend the illusion of inevitable recurrence and move confidently toward a future marked by resilience, innovation, and enlightened progress.

It is the profound testament of the pattern-seeking human spirit: not merely to observe the tides of history, but to learn to navigate them; not just to recognize the reflections in the mirror of the past, but to reshape our image in the present. In the enduring dance between chaos and order, tradition and innovation, the accurate measure of our civilization will be found not in whether we repeat cycles but in how courageously we choose to break them, forging a destiny that transcends the predictable and embodies the boundless potential of human consciousness. The future awaits, not as a pre-ordained script, but as a canvas on which we, with newfound awareness and unwavering agency, will paint the boldest, most resilient patterns yet.

About the Author

Allen Schery is a distinguished philosophical anthropologist, historian, author, educator, and museum designer whose multifaceted career embodies a deep commitment to understanding the nature of human thought, culture, and identity. With a PhD in anthropology, Allen's academic and intellectual pursuits span a broad interdisciplinary spectrum, integrating philosophy, archaeology, cultural theory, ethics, sociology, neuroscience and history to explore the fundamental questions of what it means to be human.

From the early stages of his academic journey, Allen has been fascinated by the ways humans make sense of their world—how they recognize and create patterns in behavior, symbols, language, and social structures. Pattern Seeking Ape reflects this enduring passion by providing a compelling examination of the cognitive and cultural mechanisms that underpin human existence. This work synthesizes Allen's extensive research with thoughtful reflection to offer readers both a profound theoretical framework and practical insights into human nature and our shared heritage.

In addition to Pattern Seeking Ape, Allen is the author of The Dragon's Breath, a captivating narrative that explores themes of transformation, power, and resilience through a blend of historical and mythological storytelling. This work exemplifies Allen's ability to weave complex human experiences into engaging prose, inviting readers to reflect on broader cultural and philosophical questions inspired by ancient symbolism and contemporary relevance.

Allen's scholarly contributions are marked by their clarity, depth, and interdisciplinary scope. He has authored numerous academic publications and accessible writings, always aiming to bridge the gap between specialized scholarship and public understanding. His work is informed by formal training in archaeology and anthropology, which grounds his philosophical inquiries in empirical evidence and historical context. This unique combination of theory and practice allows Allen to approach human culture with a rare and valuable perspective.

Beyond writing, Allen applies his expertise through the design and development of museums. He creates immersive educational environments that bring history and anthropology to life for diverse audiences. His museum projects are characterized by thoughtful storytelling and engagement strategies that connect visitors emotionally and intellectually with the exhibits.

As an active member of the Society for American Baseball Research (SABR) specializing in Dodger History, Allen nurtures his lifelong enthusiasm for baseball history. This passion complements his academic work, blending meticulous research techniques with a humanistic appreciation for cultural phenomena. Through this intersection of sport and scholarship, he continues to expand his understanding of American cultural identity and memory.

Allen is also a seasoned independent publisher, adept in navigating the evolving landscapes of digital and print publishing. He leverages his work through various platforms to bring his works and those of other authors to readers worldwide. His experience with book production, cover design, and formatting reflects a practical mastery of the publishing process that supports his mission to disseminate knowledge widely.

In addition to his academic and publishing pursuits, Allen maintains an active role in digital content creation, hosting a YouTube channel that provides lectures, research insights, and accessible educational material to a broader audience. Through these channels, he fosters ongoing dialogue about anthropology, history, and philosophy in the digital age.

Based Southern California, Allen embraces a lifestyle that balances intellectual rigor with personal passions. He is an aficionado of classic cars, particularly restoring Corvettes, exemplifying his appreciation for craftsmanship, history, and innovation. This balance between the analytical and the tactile shapes his holistic worldview and enriches his scholarly endeavors.

With Pattern Seeking Ape and The Dragon's Breath, Allen Schery offers readers an invitation to explore the profound cognitive patterns, cultural processes, and diverse narratives that define humanity. His work stands as a significant contribution to contemporary philosophical anthropology, encouraging a deeper understanding of ourselves as pattern-seeking beings and cultural architects. Through meticulous scholarship, clear exposition, and passionate inquiry, Allen continues to illuminate the intricate tapestry of human existence for academic and general audiences alike.

INDEX

A b Urbe Condita, 220

Abolitionist Tools, 224, 226

Aboriginal Australian cultures, 34, 53

adaptive process, 187

Age of Philip II, 220–21

Age of Revolution, 220–21

AI, 99–104, 134–35, 141, 143–44, 145, 148, 216, 224

AI models, 99–100, 103

AI systems, 102, 104, 134, 143, 145, 147

ancient patterns, 25, 36

ant colonies, 151, 155, 158

Anunnaki, 65, 67–68

archetypes, 8, 22, 90, 94, 122, 124–26, 128, 161, 196, 199

architects, 68, 117, 119, 151, 153

architecture, 11, 43, 115, 117, 118, 144, 153–54, 158, 161, 223–24, 225

neural, 5, 7, 102

artificial intelligence, 14, 47, 99, 101, 110, 133–34, 141, 172, 223, 224–25

Astrological predictions, 72, 79

astrology, 8, 69–70, 71–78, 79–81

Babylonians meticulously tracked planetary movements, 73, 80

balance, cosmic, 73, 81

Barnum Effect, 71–72, 79

Bayeux Tapestry, 71, 79

belief systems, 84, 90, 92

Believing Brain, 221

biases, 13, 15–16, 47, 57, 132, 133, 138, 169–70, 206, 217

Bishop, Christopher M., 224–25

Black Box Society, 224, 226

Boden, Margaret, 225

boundaries of time, 124, 202

brain networks, 186

Bridle, James, 224–26

Campbell, Joseph, 23, 93, 161, 221, 223–24, 225

celestial phenomena, interpretations of, 70, 77

central processing unit (CPU), 12

Chancellor, Edward, 227–28

Changing World Order, 227–28

chaos of existence, 26, 167

Chinese traditions, 73, 81

Christian tradition, 70, 77

civilizations, ancient, 21, 30, 66, 68

cognition, biological, 101

cognitive architecture, 8, 15, 48

cognitive biases, 56, 57, 71, 79, 109, 119, 132, 169, 179, 210

cognitive heuristics, 12–13

cognitive landscapes, 16

cognitive models, 183

cognitive shortcuts, 15, 170, 217

cognitive systems, 45

cognitive tendencies, 84, 109

cognitive theories, 20, 29, 52, 125

Comet, 70–71, 77–79

Convergence Culture, 225

cosmic alignment, 70, 78

Cosmic Meaning-Making, 8, 76

cosmic order, 31, 32, 35, 73, 80, 195

cosmos, 25, 26, 31–32, 37, 58, 69, 74–77, 81, 93, 107–8, 123

CPU (central processing unit), 12

Craig, Alan B., 226

Creating Narratives, 225

creation, 22–23, 31–32, 34, 64, 112, 205, 213

creative thinking, 101

creativity, artistic, 188

cross-cultural exchanges, 35

cryptids, 8, 52–54, 55–56, 57–58

Cryptozoology, 221–22

cultural landscapes, 91, 174

cycles

natural, 195

recognized patterns risks reinforcing, 171

recurring, 172–73, 205

cyclical patterns, 206, 215

Dalio, Ray, 227–28

Däniken, Von, 62, 64, 66, 68

DAOs (decentralized autonomous organizations), 153

Dawkins, Richard, 221, 222

deities, 13, 19, 22, 31–32, 34, 65

design

algorithm-generated fashion, 181

algorithmic, 148, 154

cognitive, 44

determinism, historical, 211

Diamond, Jared, 228

Dickey, Colin, 222–23

digital environments, interactive, 177

digital patterns, 154

diversity, cognitive, 6–7

dopamine, 118, 185, 190, 191

Dover Demon, 51

dreams, 8, 66, 122–29, 137, 146

personal, 127, 135, 146

early humans, 4–5, 19, 20, 22, 23, 29, 32, 84

echo chambers, digital, 54, 133

echo nature, 117

echo, timeless symbols, 146

Escher, M.C., 221

Eternal Golden Braid, 221, 225

evidence, 22, 46, 55, 62–64, 67–69, 70, 77, 84–86, 170, 199, 208, 210, 217

evolution

cognitive, 99

natural, 66

experience, subjective, 12, 102, 103

Eye of Power, 222–23

Eye's Mind, 223

Faces, 221–24, 225

Fata Morgana, 41–43

Fernand Braudel, 220

Financial History, 227–28

flexibility, cognitive, 45, 185–86, 190

Fourth Turning, 227–28

GANs (Generative Adversarial Networks), 143

Geertz, Clifford, 93, 222–24

Generative Adversarial Networks (GANs), 143

genetic engineering, 65, 67–68

Gerhard Richter, 223

Gibbon, Edward, 220

Gibson, William, 224–25

Gladwell, Malcolm, 221, 222

God pattern, 8, 36

gods, 22–24, 30–31, 33, 94, 222

growth, cognitive, 191

heavens, 30–32, 65, 69–70, 77–78

heritage, cognitive, 6, 37

hero's journey, 90, 93–95, 161, 163–64, 196

archetypal, 19, 127, 135, 146

High-Tech Tools Profile, 224, 226

historical cycles act, 209

historical patterns, 205, 216–18

History of Financial Speculation, 227–28

History of Humankind, 220

Hobsbawm, Eric, 220–21

Hofstadter, Douglas, 221, 225

Holl, Steven, 223

Howe, Neil, 227–28

human cognition, 8, 109, 140, 147

human experience, 9, 13, 124–25, 143, 161, 194, 201–2, 220

human ingenuity, 134, 137, 147, 151, 154, 156, 158

human Mind Painting, 91

human nature, 16

human pattern-seeking, 171

human psychology, 89, 167

human societies, 23, 156, 205–6, 213, 215

Humanity's Problem-Solving Engine, 8, 10

humans frame unexplained occurrences, 69, 77

Ibn Khaldun, 205, 213, 227–28

Ica stones, 63, 67, 68

illusion, 41, 47–48, 73, 80, 85, 215, 219, 221

Illusion of Progress, 9, 204, 212–13

imagery, symbolic, 25

instinct

cognitive, 27

evolutionary, 57, 83

pattern-seeking, 70, 77

intelligence, hybrid, 142, 148

Interpretation of Cultures, 222–24

Jean-Paul Sartre, 225, 227

Jesse Walker, 222–23

Juglar cycles, 207, 214

Kahneman, Daniel, 221, 222, 226–27

Kennedy, Paul, 227–28

laws, natural, 41, 158

legacy

cognitive, 25

shared human, 127

Leopold von Ranke, 220

machine algorithms, 137

machine learning models, 132, 141

manifests, computational creativity, 153

manipulation, cognitive, 86

Maya culture, 62

media, 85, 125, 164, 167, 170

Mediterranean, 220–21

Meme Machine, 223, 227

memeplexes, 92–93

Mesoamerican cultures, 33

metacognition, 9, 212–13, 217–18, 228

metacognition unveils, 218

metacognitive inquiry results, 218

mind paintings, 34, 36–37, 74, 81

Mongolian Death Worm, 51, 53

movements, celestial, 69, 71, 73–77, 79, 80

mythmaking, 4, 19–20, 21, 25–26, 61

mythologies, 24, 32, 33, 35, 37, 124

myths, cultural, 125

Napoleonic Wars and early abolition movements in North America, 70, 78

Narrative Economics, 226

narrative fallacy, 210, 217

narratives

alien, 8, 60, 64

cosmic, 64, 68, 74, 81

cosmological, 69, 77

multifaceted, 172, 218

oral, 19, 96

sacred, 30, 34–37, 197

national myths, 197, 199

Native American traditions, 53, 93

natural selection, 3

natural world, 11, 20, 22, 32–33, 36, 51, 58, 110, 151, 159

Nazca lines, 61, 67, 68

neocortex, 8, 11–12, 14–15

neuroplasticity, 185, 187–88, 190, 191

New Dark Age, 224–26

New Digital Storytelling, 225

New Frontier of Perception, 9, 176

New Jim Code, 224, 226

Niall Ferguson, 227–28

norms, cultural, 199

Novembre, Fabio, 223–24

optical illusions, 8, 41, 46–48, 221

oral traditions, ancient, 54, 56

Oswald Spengler, 206, 214, 227–28

Pakal, 62, 67, 68

pareidolia, 4, 20, 22–23, 61, 84, 99–100, 109, 119, 222

Pareidolia and Hidden Patterns in Politics, 8, 82

pattern detection, 186, 189

pattern recognition

neural networks underpinning, 190

neurochemical underpinnings of, 9, 191

pattern-recognition abilities, 45

pattern-recognition faculties, 177, 183

pattern-seeking society, 9, 166, 171–72, 174

People's History, 220

perception, machine, 99

policymakers, social, 209, 216

political polarization, 15, 169

political upheavals, 167, 215

politics, 9, 83–85, 86, 166, 205, 224

precision, cognitive, 189

prehistoric cave paintings, 195

prehistoric chronology, 63

prehistoric timeline, 63

primordial waters, 33

prophecy, 69–70, 73, 74–77, 80, 81

rapid eye movement (REM), 186

recognition, 3, 13, 99, 187

facial, 99

speech, 102

recognizing patterns, 109, 119, 172–73

recurring motifs, 123, 127, 135, 146, 207, 215

recurring patterns, 126, 169–70, 173–74, 199, 205, 208–10, 213, 217–18

religious narrative, 70, 77

structured, 69, 77

REM (rapid eye movement), 186

repeating cycles, 9, 204, 206, 210, 211–12, 218

repetition, 83, 84, 86, 115, 120, 189, 223

revolutions, digital, 91, 163

rhythms, structured, 127, 135

Riley, Bridget, 223

Roman Empire, 109, 206, 208, 214, 220

Ruha Benjamin, 224, 226

Saturn, 72, 79–80

Secret Algorithms, 224, 226

Secret Societies Shapes American Democracy, 222

Sitchin, 64–68

social media platforms, 57

spatial narratives, imaginative, 117

stagnation, cultural, 197

stimuli, complex, 23, 186

stories, unique Dreamtime, 34, 53

storytelling, cultural, 47

Strauss, William, 227–28

structured religious binaries, 74, 81

subconscious, 8, 122–24, 127, 136, 137

Sumerian terms, 65

Sumerian texts, 67–68

superheroes, 22–24, 36

symbolic systems, 67

symbolism, 64, 69, 77, 83, 127, 136, 202

cultural, 201

symbols

archetypal, 124

mystical, 109, 119

Tacitus, 220

technological associations, 64

technological landscapes, 156

technological patterns, 9, 150, 158

technological precision intertwine, 164

technology

advanced, 61, 64

digital, 13, 197

immersive, 181–83

Teutonic Nations, 220

themes, 30, 32–33, 64, 90, 94–95, 170, 174, 209

thinking, 8, 143, 171, 218, 221, 222, 226–27

timeless narrative structures, 90, 164

tools, neurocognitive, 36

Toynbee, Arnold J., 206, 214, 227–28

traditions, 52, 92, 120, 174, 197–98, 199, 201, 210, 219

transcending, 124–26, 173

transformation, 19, 32, 34, 93–94, 99, 138, 146, 147, 195, 198, 201–2, 209, 218 trends, historical, 217

Trump, 85–86

Two:Cognitive Architecture, 10

unconscious, 126, 135, 137, 144

universal patterns, 161, 172

universe, 19, 25, 32, 38, 58, 69, 73–77, 81, 107, 112, 118, 195

unpredictability, 109, 111, 113, 116, 119, 144, 145, 174, 195

validation, 89–91

Virginia Eubanks, 224, 226

Virtual Reality, immersive, 163, 164

visual artifacts, 64, 66

Visual Expression, 8, 114

visual recognition, 100

Waldo, 45, 47

warnings, 20, 56, 70–71, 78, 168, 218

William, 71, 78–79

Yuval Noah Harari, 220

Zinn, Howard, 220

Made in the USA
Monee, IL
29 September 2025